What to Expect for 2015 and Beyond

Expanded Edition

Prophet Anthony Starnes

Starnesxyz@Yahoo.com

authorHOUSE®

AuthorHouse™
1663 Liberty Drive
Bloomington, IN 47403
www.authorhouse.com
Phone: 1 (800) 839-8640

Published by AuthorHouse 08/14/2015

ISBN: 978-1-5049-2023-0 (sc)
ISBN: 978-1-5049-2022-3 (e)

Library of Congress Control Number: 2015910432

Scripture quotations marked KJV are from the Holy Bible, King James Version (Authorized Version). First published in 1611. Quoted from the KJV Classic Reference Bible, Copyright © 1983 by The Zondervan Corporation.

Scripture quotations marked AMP are from *The Amplified Bible*, Old Testament copyright © 1965, 1987 by the Zondervan Corporation. *The Amplified Bible*, New Testament copyright © 1954, 1958, 1987 by The Lockman Foundation. Used by permission. All rights reserved.

Swaggart, Jimmy. The Expositor's Study Bible: King James Version. Baton Rouge, LA: 2005. Print.

Print information available on the last page.

Any people depicted in stock imagery provided by Thinkstock are models, and such images are being used for illustrative purposes only. Certain stock imagery © Thinkstock.

This book is printed on acid-free paper.

Because of the dynamic nature of the Internet, any web addresses or links contained in this book may have changed since publication and may no longer be valid. The views expressed in this work are solely those of the author and do not necessarily reflect the views of the publisher, and the publisher hereby disclaims any responsibility for them.

Table of Contents

Introduction

Although this book concerns Christian End Time Prophecy, it is not about an esoteric eschatology so much as the hidden issues of the day. This book discloses truths that God wants known. As an example, the ever increasing deficit comes about in part from the throwing out of free spying by Christian Prophets in favor of expensive secular 'military industrial' spying of spy satellites, wire tapping of phones, computer hacking, tapping into the internet and cell phones, and drones complete with 'octopus' agencies like Homeland Security, FEMA, NSA, TSA, CIA, FBI, ATF and IRS keeping their eyes on every move you make thanks to your taxes.

This came about during the cold war when former president Eisenhower used to visit a Christian Prophet in Pasadena, California about once each month to find out what God saw behind the 'iron curtain'. His advisors told him that his policy was relying too much on Christianity and the Christian Prophets. So they encouraged him to acquire a more 'military industrial' means of spying like the new U2 spy plane. Eisenhower adopted this idea but it blew up in his face as the U2 spy plane was shot down over the Soviet Union and its pilot, Francis Gary Powers was held hostage. Nevertheless this policy grew along with your taxes.

Today the Soviet Union has fallen apart but now America not only spies on other nations with these technological instruments but on its own citizens as well and also lies about it all.

Muslims like Obama are allowed by their lies thanks to Muslim false doctrine to conceal, disguise and hide their personal beliefs, Ideas, feelings and opinions about anything and everything in order to achieve personal success for the Muslim cause. Like ruling over Christians or even hiring other Muslims like Valerie Jarrett as public

employees to abuse Christians and promote Iran's nuclear arms as well.

To make my disclosure about Muslim lying clearer, it must be reiterated that as long as a Muslim is in a country where Islam is a minority, then the Muslim (in this case, Obama) deceptiveness about anything is officially expected and sanctioned by the 'evil religion of Islam' (the Muslim faith). That's why we should throw all the Muslims out!

In any case all should now see clearly that the Black man 'Duncan' who lied about not being exposed to EBOLA in order to get on the plane and come to America also died here as 'the wages of sin is death'. But he only told one lie. What judgment now awaits Obama and his many czars for telling thousands of lies about 'everything under the sun' to the American people in six years in office?

My suppressed book also reveals that the fluoridation of public drinking waters is dumbing down and effeminizing our people. Fluoride was first used as a chemical weapon by the Nazis. It was used in the drinking water of their death camps to render their inmates docile and incoherent (so they could not fight back). This is now being used in your tap water to secretly induce you to accept intermarrying and the political propaganda of the day (Muslim Obama's anti American Muslim socialist agenda including gay marriage).

My other issues discussed include extra terrestrial aliens, the smallpox genocide of Indians, high fructose corn syrup making Americans obese, banks being bailed out since they're 'too big to fail' while you lose your homes to foreclosure and wind up homeless with food stamps. **Dumping Christianity has bequeathed America to deceptions, wars, delusions, deficits and disasters. Watch out!**

Dedication

The three kings of Israel, Judah and Edom sought counsel from the Lord regarding a war with Moab in II Kings 3: 11, 12. So they called for the prophet Elisha. Who said 'bring me a minstrel' (II Kings 3:15), so he could get a word from God.

Over the years these minstrels have helped me get this word from God for you.

Vestal Goodman of 'The Happy Goodman's'

The Original Jesus Movement singers

The Original Maranatha Singers

The Bill Gaither Singers

The original singers of John Wimber's
Vineyard in Anaheim, California

My distant relative; the anointed singer John Starnes

Jimmy Swaggart's Family Worship Center Singers

And the anointed singer Nancy Harman.

Since Wars are coming then Famines, Pestilences and Earthquakes composing 'The Beginnings of Sorrows' according to the prophecy of the Lord Jesus (Matthew 24:6-8) I got inspired by these minstrels in this exact Biblical method to receive this word from God for you, your safety and your well being.

Acknowledgments

I want to express my Appreciation first to my speller, typist and all around accomplished assistant in this grueling task: Patrick McClenahen.

And the staff of the Volusia County Library Center at City Island in Daytona Beach, Florida who kept their old public computers up and running like new to keep my manuscript legible enough for publication.

Preface

Most Christians have been taught that the Christian experience begins by faith. Even the Bible teaches that **'the just shall live by faith' (Galatians 3:11).** But without a spark from God generated by the Holy Ghost, Christians cannot **'move on into the high calling of God' (Philippians 3:14).**

Likewise here in America most cars run on gasoline but they are not started by it. They must be started by a spark generated by a catalytic converter in order to start the engine to burn the gas to move the car. Even if a car's gas tank is full of gas it's not going to move without a spark to burn the gas.

Today, we have many Christians who know their Bible verses well and the words to the songs sung in church too but because they have not received the spark of the Holy Ghost they do not move on to do God's will or even to both adequately understand and apply what those Bible verses they learned mean in their lives and with current events. Thus the Christian divorce rate is about the same as that of non-Christians and Christians who believe in life nevertheless vote for abortionist Democrats. **'Brethren these things ought not so to be' (James 3:10).**

I just become a senior citizen, so I suppose that it's time for me to write my autobiography, Christian commentary on current events and end time prophecy. So I will tell the whole truth and nothing but the truth whether it's liked or not.

After I mentioned my few accomplishments in this life and gave my testimony, the Lord suddenly stopped me and said: **'you've said enough about yourself to let the people know who you are and Whose you are. Now that you've given your personal introduction, I want you to say what I want said. From now on your book will move from being just another autobiography to a no-nonsense Christian commentary. And more than just a controversial Christian** commentary but also an end time prophecy that I intend to send exactly what the Lord Jesus prophesied first Deceptions, then Wars, then Famines, Pestilences and Earthquakes just as it is written, so shall it be done'.

My Autobiography

Back when I had just become a teenager my dad gave me his old family Victrola complete with some old records from his family in Virginia. Some of these old records were gospel songs of famous quartets like 'The Carter family','The Chuck Wagon Gang' and 'The Smokey Mountain Boys'. Of course that type of music was different from what we heard over the radio back then and even now.

I grew up in a typical middleclass neighborhood on Mulberry Street in Daytona Beach, Florida. Mulberry Street is on the mainland side of town, east of US 1, west of Beach Street and the part we lived on was south of Madison Ave.

My family never went to church so neither did I. Therefore I grew up American pagan. But one day I stopped by a church in our neighborhood. These church people were singing old fashioned gospel songs just like I heard from that old Victrola my dad gave me. This church was of a holiness denomination called the First Church of the Nazarene. They had a song leader who was a very big man. He was both very tall and very heavy; he must have weighed over 400lbs, and he had a booming voice.

Sometimes I would stop by that church when they were singing. The song leader, that big man, would tell them the page number of the song and hum the key so that the congregation could start to sing. But once he started singing too, no one could hear anyone else but him. His voice carried up and down the street and even across the street. **His singing somehow made me shake;** I liked the feeling even though I did not fully understand it back then. Folks in the neighborhood said that he was an anointed singer set apart by God with the gift of praise. Others said that he was the only truly sanctified man that they had ever seen. In any case this was the first time I ever felt God. No one had ever told me that it was even possible to feel God. So I must have had that old 'hard shell, hog and hominy' Baptist belief drilled into me; that any religious experience or relationship with God was based on rules, regulations and laws of scripture or faith that one just accepted as true instead of any feelings at all.

Around the same time a TV Program came on the air each week called: 'The Happy Goodman's'. They sang the same old gospel tunes that that church sang. So I thought that that same feeling like exhilaration with shaking might happen again as the wife of the evangelist, Vestal Goodman also sang with an anointed voice. **By this time I had learned by experience that the anointing on others somehow made me shake.** One day they described how this anointing had come on Vestal.

Vestal Goodman and her husband Howard were holding revivals in a small town in Louisiana. A bad hurricane had come through, torn the tent and things up and rained all over the electrical equipment so that they had no working microphone. Vestal got up to sing anyway by faith with her soft soprano voice. Just then the Holy Spirit came upon her and her voice boomed throughout that tattered tent, everyone heard her. Her shocked family was astonished and asked what had happened. An old woman replied that the Spirit of God had just anointed her with power to do what God wanted done.

Since that day the fame of this woman and her voice has gone throughout the land and even onto television, which was just black and white back in those days. Although I was still not yet a born again Christian, nevertheless I watched that show religiously every week because it made me feel good and I got to shake just like a 'holy roller' even though I was just an unsaved street kid.

About that same time, a Baptist evangelist who drove a new Cadillac car put up a big tent to hold revival in Holly Hill, Florida, the town next door. I remember that his tent was put up in a swampy area which is now filled in and has luxury homes built there. I guess those people living in those luxury homes would be horrified to know that their expensive homes were built on filled in swamp.

These Baptist people sang those same gospel tunes, but without any feeling in them. Nevertheless I went forward to get saved anyway since I wanted to get closer to God in order to shake. But since there was no feeling in that experience and I never shook there, it did not seem to last.

It lasted a little while though and I even got adopted by a well to do childless couple named O'Brien who took me to every Sunday service at White Chapel Church of God where I was baptized in water in 1961. But since there was no feeling there in time I fell away into naughtiness, common to the street life I grew up in. Gradually my bad behavior sank into open sin. In time I was convicted of forgery and sent away to serve a couple of years in the Florida State Prison. But then my second chance to experience God and shake 'big-time' began right in that prison.

This was really weird but before I share it, let me describe my prison experience first. At first I was somewhat apprehensive because I was a good looking former surfer with blonde hair. Back then I was already a high school graduate with some college and could also type, therefore the classification supervisor of the Florida prison system had me become his new clerk. This was a trustee position complete with a white uniform and a special pass to go anywhere in the prison without having to be guarded.

My prison job involved my assembling of all important papers on each new inmate for the classification committee. Only free people, employees of the State of Florida get to do that same kind of work now. But back in those days I got to do it. These papers I had to acquire and assemble included official court commitment papers with any pre-sentence investigation reports or probation and parole papers, psychological reports made by the prison psychologist including IQ tests, social reports of the classification officer, chaplain's report and custody recommendation of the prison guards and whatever else was pertinent to that particular case including ID pictures and all demographic data.

Working with these papers required personal trust. I was not allowed to disclose whatever I saw. I remember one strange case that appalled me back then and still troubles me some as I wonder how a person created in the image of God could possibly do such an evil act. I'm talking about a young Black man who told everyone that he got twenty years for robbery when the court commitment papers showed he had sexually assaulted an infant by sticking his finger into her. If I had ventured to set the record straight, that guy's life would have been forfeit and I did not want his blood on my hands so I kept my mouth shut.

Otherwise this prison job was just like any other nine to five office job. Only we also had to work sometimes on weekends like Saturday or Sunday because the classification committee which met every week had to have their papers ready for them so they could decide which rehabilitation program to put each new inmate in, which correctional center to send them to and what custody was most appropriate for their rehabilitation.

A few months after I arrived it was already time for Easter. Since I had been a surfer on the outside, I was used to getting up early. So I went to Easter Sunrise Service which was one of my trusty privileges. Since this was the only day of the year when we could get out of our cells early in the morning many trustees came from all over the prison not only for the Easter service but also to remember what early mornings with sunrise was like.

Once we filled up the bleachers set up in the prison yard the Chaplain prayed. Down in front was a visiting prison chain gang dressed in prison blues. I thought that they had come to worship with us too. Instead one of their guards set down his rifle and introduced one of them to sing for us. This singer was a young Black man who started to sing the old Negro Spiritual about 'Sometimes It Causes Me to Tremble'. At once I recognized that this man had a professional voice, since I had studied voice in college and knew that his voice had a three octave range. In other words, he could hit any note in music both low notes and high ones too. So I wondered why a guy with such a fabulous voice, better than anyone I had ever heard was in prison with the rest of us, just cutting grass on the side of some road every day. Then my mind moved from being centered on his voice to the words of the song he sang for us. As he finished singing the first verse he went on to sing the chorus about 'Sometimes It Causes Me to Tremble' and **I started to shake uncontrollably again just as I had done before as a kid.**

This time my shaking was 'big time'. As it would not stop. One of my friends gave me my prison jacket but I still shook since I really wasn't cold. **Usually I had learned by experience that my shaking accompanied someone's anointing and when their anointing was over, my shaking ended too**. But this time I shook after that Black man finished singing and for the rest of that Easter Sunrise service. I shook on the way back to our cells too. Once we arrived I still shook. I even shook for count time that morning. When I went to eat breakfast I still shook. It's hard to eat when you're shaking but somehow I managed to eat my oatmeal.

Afterward, since it was a holiday and I did not have to work, I returned to my housing area and laid down to take a nap. But I could not go to sleep as I still shook. By this time my shaking had gone from just my usual feeling good about my shaking to concern and even alarm for my well being now.

Then it came lunch time. We all lined up to go to lunch. I still shook but I was determined to eat this good holiday meal anyway. The lunchroom people had prepared Black Angus steaks from the prison farm for us. These steaks were big, juicy and filled the whole plate. So big that our vegetables had to be put on top of our steaks. Actually all this food was both very fresh and very good back in those days. Eating good was seen to be a basic human right even for prison inmates back then. So the steaks were real, without soy fillers. The State of Florida had a huge Division of Corrections farm and ranch in Belle Glade, Florida from whence our food came.

As we sat down to eat people avoided sitting by me as if I were contaminated with some sickness that they were afraid to catch, since I still shook but I managed to eat my steak anyway.

After eating our group of inmates returned to our dorm to watch TV sports. But I laid down to take an afternoon nap. Since I was still shaking I could not go to sleep. So after a few hours of self imposed rest I got up to get ready for supper.

At supper I sat at a corner table by myself since I was still shaking. As the other guys came in they sat together at the main tables in the center. I don't remember what we ate for that meal but I'm sure it must have been good. After we ate we returned to the dorm where most of us watched the TV news. I saw the TV news too then some wrestling program.

Suddenly count time crept up on us. We all stood by our beds as the prison guard would call out our last names and we responded with our prison number. When he got to me, He called my last name; Starnes and I responded; 020,563. You never forget your prison number. Then before moving on to the next bed, he asked me if I was still shaking. I said; 'Yes Sir'. You can't hide your personal problems from the guards since it's their job to stay fully informed about those they're guarding. Then he took out a pad of colored papers and wrote me out a sick pass and told me; 'If you're still shaking in the morning be sure you make sick call. There's a bad flu going around that's killing people and we don't want you to cheat the State of Florida out of its time'. I said; 'Yes Sir' then he moved on.

I thought later that his statement to me was rather cold. But I had learned by this time to always treat prison guards with respect and common courtesy.

After count time was over we all got into our beds. Then the guard turned off our light. I tried to go to sleep but my shaking wouldn't quit. Eventually my shaking seemed to subside enough for me to go to sleep. So I slept well that night. The next morning as I woke up I noticed that my shaking was gone. Of course this all was a mystery to me back then. So I just put it out of my mind and went on doing whatever I had to face that day.

I did wonder a few times about the gospel singer at that Easter Sunrise Service if I'd ever hear his voice again. It's now been almost 50 years and I wonder whatever happened to that guy.

Once I had to go over to the photographer to retrieve some ID pictures for the Classification Committee. While there I saw the prison photographer taking ID photos of a death row inmate. Because this guy was about my same age back then and I saw on his court commitment papers under the word: sentence the word: DEATH in capital letters. So I could not look at the guy as a cold feeling would come over me. Just then the devil seemed to say that this is what happened to that singer. But I knew better as death row inmates stay on death row under maximum security, they do not work on chain gangs nor go out to sing.

My life was rather uneventful and went on normally from that day. A few months later I received an official letter from the Florida Probation and Parole Commission in Tallahassee, Florida. They told me what they were going to do and what would be happening to me. They also ordered my classification boss to have me transferred to minimum security at the Avon Park Correctional Institution in Avon Park, Florida in preparation for my release.

They said that my family had moved to California and had even found me a job out there. So they were going to give me an interstate parole, which was rare back in those days. First they would send me to Avon Park Correctional Institution for a few months of minimum custody. Then I would be released on parole to California. I was to be given bus fair to Tampa, Florida. Then fly nonstop to LA. There I would meet my folks and go to work that week. The next week I was to report to my California parole officer who would meet me at home so he could check out my living arrangements, meet my folks and interview me there in person.

When I left the Florida state prison and arrived at Avon Park Correctional Institution the first thing I noticed was the quality of the food. It seemed to me that good food was used to pacify those hoodlums, thugs and lowlifes at the main prison but not wasted on the older career criminals and white collar criminals of Avon Park Correctional Institution.

I thought that my job skills at the main prison would ease me into some type of office job. But in prison you don't get to choose what you want. You do what they need done. Back then they needed another tailor to work with the sewing machine. Of course I knew nothing about sewing but I learned quickly.

This correctional institution was much different from what I had become used to. There were less Black inmates there and much older inmates. This correctional institution also included the prison hospital, so there were some amputees and some in wheelchairs too.

Usually I keep to myself but there a middle aged Jewish inmate from South Florida became my friend. He was a very sarcastic New York Jew and conman with an unusual ability to read people like books. One day I showed him my letter from the Parole Board. After he read it, he unexpectedly broke down and told me that these people were giving me a second chance and I should feel very blessed to be given a brand new life.

After serving a few months there it was time for my release, everything happened just as the parole board had authorized. First I was dismissed from my prison job. Then sent back to my dorm to put my few personal things and papers into a plastic bag. There ordered to strip my bed and take my sheets and blanket to the laundry room. After I turned in my bedding there I was ordered to take off my prison clothes. I was then given street clothes including a new suit complete with black shoes.

After I changed into the new street clothes and returned my old prison clothes I boarded their prison bus bond for the local Greyhound bus station. There I gave them my ticket to Tampa,

Florida. Once I arrived in Tampa I went to their airport there and gave them my direct non-stop ticket for flight to LA. (Even though I was an ex-offender on parole there was no TSA in those days with all their bureaucratic searching of you and your baggage to prevent terrorism. See how much freedom we have lost.) After I boarded the plane I strapped myself in. The plane trip only took a few hours and since we crossed several time zones it was still morning when I arrived in LA.

After the plane landed I headed for the noisy terminal to meet my folks. When I stepped into that big terminal in LA, California it was like a whole new world. I had landed right into The Jesus Movement Revival complete with deliverances, healings and other Pentecostal manifestations of God's grace. Of course, I was very surprised to see with my own eyes the book of Acts coming back to life right in a public place, not a church. All sorts of ministry and other things were happening there. People were praying, crying, hollering, shouting, talking and even singing. Deliverances were happening and hands were being laid on some with miracle manifestations. Anyway there was just pandemonium there. My folks saw me and my mother got me out of there with my bag of stuff. But before we left I saw one of those Jesus people by the door handing out cards to their church and I grabbed one and stuck it in with my other personal papers and stuff.

Once I got home and unwound some and went through some debriefing I asked about these Jesus people. I was told that these people were very famous and were even on the TV news because of all the genuine stuff that they were doing and the truth that they lived as a major contrast to all the political lies about the Vietnam War. These people were mainly ex-dopers who God had forgiven and anointed to speak and do what politicians should be saying and doing. Anyway it was an 'out of sight' scene. That night I was glad to take my first bath at home. The next morning I got up early as usual to get ready to go to my new job.

My work site was a small machine shop in another town that I had to drive to. (My mother let me use her new car). I was very careful driving but it was hard after a couple of years of not driving at all. In other words I was out of practice.

Once I got there and met my new boss he told me that my new job involved me having to stand all day drilling parts for airplanes that had to be exact. I was used to office work, then sewing. I had never worked in a machine shop before. I was required to stand all day in front of a drill press and pull it down to make my little metal hole that this part needed. This was very exacting work and required occasional inspection by the owner to see that each part I did met its specifications.

The owner of the shop stayed with me that first day to insure that I did things right. His son also worked in the shop with several other men. The job was a good job and paid well. After working there that first day I drove home to eat my spaghetti dinner. (My mother is Italian and a good cook).

After we ate we watched some TV news, where we saw the Jesus people again at the airport. Then I helped my sister do her homework and went to bed. The next day I went to work again and settled into a daily routine.

'The Jesus Movement'

In time my parole ended and I got a better job that paid more where my mother worked. Since I now had the weekend free, I decided to check out that Jesus Movement Church. I had to drive there as it was in another town. As I pulled in their parking lot, I heard them singing those same old gospel songs that I first heard on the old family Victoria that my dad had given me when I first became a teenager. I felt comfortable so I went in and found a seat although it was crowded. After the singing ended and their evangelist gave his sermon it was time to pray. Since I was already a nominal Christian and knew more Bible than they did since I came from the Bible belt, I didn't think that I needed much prayer since God was already blessing me big time. Why ask for more, if you have much?

But I went down to the altar to pray anyway even though I felt that I didn't have any real needs since God was already blessing me and I felt thankful. So while I was thanking God in English, suddenly I began to thank God in other tongues too. (Now at this time there had been no mention of the baptism in the Holy Ghost). So at first I didn't really understand what had just happened. Until a few minutes later when **I started to shake again just as I had done as a teenager.** Then things came together as I figured out that my shaking had something to do with God. The Pastor of their fellowship also seemed to recognize that God was all over me and motioned me to pray for another young man nearby. Which I moved over to do and that guy began to speak in tongues too. Well it was all wonderful and I drove home thanking God. But I still did not fully understand it.

I first learned on subsequent visits to their church that these Jesus people were mainly of two different types. Most, especially the regular worshippers were native Californians. Other Jesus people were transients from everywhere and anywhere. The native Californians were more educated and more middle class than most Americans. They were the all white children of California aerospace workers. They were not racially diverse but still had revival anyway.

13

The next Sunday I visited that church again. After service and praying some it was time to go to Katherine Khulman's miracle crusade that afternoon in downtown LA. I went because I liked to see God doing stuff. I guess I went several times. Her meeting was held in the Shrine auditorium in downtown LA, once each month back in the late 1960's and early 1970's.

Once I happened to arrive late at one of her meeting. So I was at the entrance, way down in back trying to find a seat like everyone else. Katharine Khulman was far away up on the stage. The service had just started and they had sung her theme songs about 'Believing in Miracles' and 'He Touched Me'. As the songs ended, she stopped the service and pointed to where I was standing and said that the Holy Ghost was doing something back there where I was. Some of the women by me started shrieking. We all looked to see what was happening. We saw a young woman with a red dot on her forehead (apparently a Hindu) carrying a baby that had water on the brain with a head as big as a watermelon. As we looked at the baby's head I guess our vision became like what the dopers call 'trails' or intermittent vision. Anyway we saw the baby's head shrink in stages from watermelon size down to the size of a football right in front of our eyes. This was the most 'out of sight' miracle that I ever personally saw. It caused some of us who realized that we were now in the presence of the living God to fall on our faces. Thank You, Jesus

The next Sunday I went to that Jesus people church again and found out that it was called Bethel Tabernacle, founded by the pastor Lyle Steenis of the California Evangelical Association. It was full gospel but not part of any Pentecostal Denomination. It was not a teaching church with programs. Instead it was a Spirit filled independent deliverance church. They took most scriptures literally. **It seemed that their main concern was to get new converts baptized in the Holy Spirit. Since the ex-dopers there believed in feeling and had taken dope for that purpose, they insisted that one's conversion and**

salvation was not complete without feeling God in Holy Spirit baptism. And once one was baptized in the Holy Spirit they did not need any man to teach them **(1 John 2:27).** This seemed to work out well as I never saw any of them arguing about anything. No one ever seemed to raise their voice and I never saw any fights there.

Although I was neither a native Californian nor an ex-doper these Jesus people wanted me to move in with them and become part of their ministry of evangelism and miracles. They seemed to recognize that I knew more Bible than they did. But this was because I was from the Bible belt of the South. Where almost all of us know a whole lot more Bible than what we really live out in our daily lives. Since I had also always been a loner to some degree I was reluctant about moving in and told them I'd pray about it.

I knew that these people also prayed about things first before they did them, so I figured that this must be God and I moved in and went where they went all over Southern California ministering.

Looking back on it all now, I spent the best three years of my life there and I thank God that I was given the privilege and the high honor to give to the Lord Jesus the best three years of my life, from age 20 to 23. And I was not yet wheelchair disabled back then.

I moved into one of their apartments. (That church owned several apartments). I had my own room in one of them. My days were very busy. We did not read devotions, we lived them. Sometimes we'd get to pray before we ate. Sometimes we didn't even have enough time to eat. Each day began with me going with big AL on his flatbed truck to obtain groceries for the beloved. We got that food by 'dumpster diving', eating for free what the supermarkets had thrown away. Our job was to keep five separate rehabilitation homes supplied with good food. We always had enough and sometimes we gave good food away at the church or on the street or at the beach or at the airport.

Every Sunday Pastor Steenis, the old dirt farmer from Kansas would give us our 'Marching orders' via his sermon for that week. One Sunday he told us that he had heard about a new book about the end times that some of us were reading. This book was entitled: <u>The Late Great Planet Earth</u> by Hal Lindsey.

He went on to tell us that 'Hal Lindsey had been a student at Dallas Theological Seminary, a Baptist school in Texas and had just published information taken from his class notes in his eschatology class. The pre-tribulation rapture was a common heretical Baptist Viewpoint which Hal Lindsey had presented as his own. Such plagiarism and calling it revelation is theft. And theft does not authenticate any theology especially Revelation. Moreover no Baptist who doesn't even believe that the gifts of the Holy Spirit are for today could possibly receive the Gift of Revelation required to write a True Prophetic Book.

Now we're gonna sing a song for a few moments while you all can get some pencils and pens and notepads to take notes to write down these Three Words of Wisdom that will blow away this Pre-Tribulation Rapture heresy.

The Pre-Tribulation Rapture heresy began with notes from the old Scofield Reference Bible some of us used in Kansas when I was a kid. Remember as our preacher told us back then: 'the Bible is inspired, but Scofield's notes are not'. The Bible says in **Ecclesiastes 4:12 'That a threefold cord is not easily broken'**, so here are your Three Words of Wisdom: 1. At Revelation 4:1 the deceived say that the whole church is called to come up. (As in the Pre-Tribulation Rapture heresy). But the scripture only calls the Prophet John up to be shown or given a road map about the future. This type of impartation is typical of prophets in receiving revelatory words from God that Baptists know nothing about. 2. **The 'trumpet' in Revelation 4:1 is not the same as the last trumpet of first Corinthians 15:51, 52.**

Let's read **Revelation 4:1 'After this I looked, and, behold, a door was opened in heaven: and the first voice which I heard was as it were a trumpet talking with me; which said, COME UP HITHER AND I WILL SHOW THEE THINGS, WHICH MUST BE HEREAFTER'.** And **1 Corinthians 15:52 'In a moment, in the twinkling of an eye at the last trump: for the trumpet shall sound, and the dead shall be raised incorruptible, and we shall be changed'.** In the first trumpet John is shown the future but in the last trump we are changed to handle it. And 3.There is no mention of saints but only angels around the thrown of God in the rest of Revelation Chapter 4. If the saints had been raptured they'd be mentioned as being somewhere up there, as you can read and see for yourself.

I think that I have made my point, I could go on by saying that this false doctrine was the pet of the Christian elite just like the common capitalist practice of exploitation which says; 'get what you can get while the getting is good then get out'. Only the Christians that are into prosperity say: 'get what you can get while the getting is good and then God will get us out'.

Many capitalist investors and farmers once believed this same foolish theory but they saw their money lose value, their stocks fall and the depression still come anyway. Good farmland became dust and blew away. We lived in Kansas and saw part of Oklahoma blow our way, it happen right before our eyes.

Someone once said that the Bible is a road map from here to heaven. If so, no map has ever described in detail an eventful trip that no one really needs to know about since they won't ever be around to take it anyway, since they'll already be gone. **Revelation is included in the Bible roadmap because it's part of the trip that we're all gonna take someday**. And taking any trip instantly, secretly and on impulse without proper preparation and following its prescribed order is folly. **The prescribed order is in Matthew 24** which you can read yourself after we pray. Are there any questions? If not it's time to pray'.

After we prayed for some to get saved and to receive the baptism in the Holy Spirit, some of us discussed what the pastor had shared.

Two wealthy Jewish girls who lived up the hill from the church in Palos Verdes said that Hal Lindsey also lived up there with the rich. Apparently he had written that book to help fund his lavish lifestyle up there. In other words his book from his college notes was seen as a wise entrepreneurial play by some, especially Jewish investors. But that same book composed of false prophecy was being used as a scam on the Christian community.

But Hal Lindsey had one good thing going for him. Some of his opponents, critics and others called him a Christian Zionist. If so that probably aided his prosperity so much so that he really didn't need to write this book to raise funds.

When considering nourishment and insight from his ministry, I believe that Christians should eat the fish but spit out the bones. His pre-tribulation rapture heresy should thus be spit out. But Hal Lindsey has made a few good points of insightful knowledge especially in his TV program to benefit both the Christian community and informed voters by publically rebuking anti-Semitic acts of these foolish politicians that bring God's judgment upon America. I'll just list a few:

1. On October 30, 1991 the then Republican President George H. W. Bush, (Bush 41), opened the Madrid conference about the land of Israel for Middle East Peace. A rebuke from the God of Israel in the form of a storm sent 35 ft waves to cause significant damage to President Bush's Kennebunkport, Maine home.

2. On January 16, 1994 the then Democratic President Bill Clinton met with the Syrian President to discuss land for peace, about Israel surrendering the Golan Heights. Within 24 hours the powerful 6.9 Northridge earthquake rocked Southern California.

3. Especially for you environmentalists: on April 19, 2010 the Democratic President Obama told the UN that the US no longer would automatically side with Israel at the UN. Within 24 hours of Muslim sympathizer President Obama's statement an explosion causing British Petroleum's oil rig disaster in the Gulf of Mexico resulting in the multibillion dollar Gulf of Mexico oil environmental catastrophe happened.

After showing us so much truth that the liberal press fails to report, Hal Lindsey manages to still show us support for his pre-tribulation rapture heresy. Some may feel that the word: 'heresy' is too strong a word to describe the pre-tribulation rapture.

But when someone's belief directly opposes the clear teaching of the Lord Jesus Christ, it ceases to be just a matter of opinion but has now become heresy. For the Lord Jesus Christ in describing his revelation or coming again says in Matthew 24:29 'Immediately AFTER the tribulation of those days...', To then say that: 'before the tribulation Jesus comes again' instead of 'AFTER ' like the Lord Jesus really said is not just twisting the truth but 'bearing false witness' worse than heresy. All heresy does contain a small measure of truth however so that it will be easily accepted as being so.

For example: The Bible says in 1 John 1:1 'In the beginning was the Word, and the Word was with God, and the Word was God'. But to the Jehovah's Witness; Jesus the Word was just 'a' god and nothing more.

Having studied Greek at Fuller Theological Seminary, the original language in which the New Testament was written, It is clearly shown that the definite article in Greek is usually translated 'the' as you can see from the word: 'the' in this phrase. But the definite article is also used in Greek to also determine which part of the phrase is subject and which part is predicate. Since the definite article has already been used to signify that

'Word' is subject, the predicate: 'God' can now have no definite article, thus no 'a' before God.

Back at Bethel Tabernacle we went on to read **Matthew 24** and found our own few words of wisdom. At the start of this chapter the Lord Jesus disciples said in Verse 3: 'Tell us when shall these things be? And what will be the sign of your coming and of the end of the age?' The Lord Jesus answered by saying: **Matthew 24:5-30:** Verse 5: 'FOR MANY SHALL COME IN MY NAME, SAYING, I AM CHRIST; AND SHALL DECIEVE MANY. Verse 6: AND YE SHALL HEAR OF WARS AND RUMORS OF WARS: SEE THAT YE BE NOT TROUBLED: FOR ALL THESE THINGS MUST COME TO PASS, BUT THE END IS NOT YET. Verse 7: FOR NATION SHALL RISE AGAINST NATION AND KINGDOM AGAINST KINGDOM: AND THERE SHALL BE FAMINES, AND PESTILENCES, AND EARTHQUAKES, IN DIVERSE PLACES. Verse 8: ALL THESE ARE THE BEGINNINGS OF SORROWS. Verse 9: THEN SHALL THEY DELIVER YOU UP TO BE AFLICTED AND SHALL KILL YOU: AND YE SHALL BE HATED OF ALL NATIONS FOR MY NAME'S SAKE. Verse 10: AND THEN SHALL MANY BE OFFENDED, AND SHALL BETRAY ONE ANOTHER, AND SHALL HATE ONE ANOTHER. Verse 11: AND MANY FALSE PROPHETS SHALL RISE, AND SHALL DECIEVE MANY. Verse 12: AND BECAUSE INIQUITY SHALL ABOUND, THE LOVE OF MANY SHALL WAX COLD. Verse 13: BUT HE THAT SHALL ENDURE UNTO THE END, THE SAME SHALL BE SAVED. Verse 14: AND THIS GOSPEL OF THE KINGDOM SHALL BE PREACHED IN ALL THE WORLD FOR A WITNESS UNTO ALL NATIONS; AND THEN SHALL THE END COME. Verse 15: WHEN YE THEREFORE SHALL SEE THE ABOMINATION OF DESOLATION, SPOKEN OF BY DANIEL THE PROPHET, STAND IN THE HOLY PLACE (WHO SO READITH, LET HIM UNDERSTAND). Verse 16: THEN LET THEM WHICH BE IN JUDEA FLEE INTO THE MOUNTAINS. Verse 17: LET HIM WHICH IS ON THE HOUSETOP NOT COME DOWN TO TAKE ANYTHING OUT OF HIS HOUSE: Verse 18: NEITHER LET HIM WHICH IS IN THE FIELD RETURN BACK TO TAKE HIS CLOTHES. Verse 19:

AND WOE UNTO THEM THAT ARE WITH CHILD, AND TO THEM THAT GIVE SUCK IN THOSE DAYS! Verse 20: BUT PRAY YE THAT YOU'RE FLIGHT BE NOT IN WINTER, NEITHER ON THE SABBATH DAY. Verse 21: FOR THEN SHALL BE GREAT TRIBULATION, SUCH AS WAS NOT SINCE THE BEGINNING OF THE WORLD TO THIS TIME, NO, NOR EVER SHALL BE. Verse 22: AND EXCEPT THOSE DAYS SHOULD BE SHORTENED THERE SHOULD NO FLESH BE SAVED: BUT FOR THE ELECT'S SAKE THOSE DAYS SHALL BE SHORTENED. Verse 23: THEN IF ANY MAN SHALL SAY UNTO YOU, LO, HERE IS CHRIST, OR THERE: BELIEVE IT NOT. Verse 24: FOR THERE SHALL ARISE FALSE CHRISTS, AND FALSE PROPHETS, AND SHALL SHOW GREAT SIGNS AND WONDERS, INSOMUCH THAT, IF IT WERE POSSIBLE, THEY SHALL DECIEVE THE VERY ELECT. Verse 25: BEHOLD, I HAVE TOLD YOU BEFORE. Verse 26: WHEREFORE IF THEY SHALL SAY UNTO YOU, BEHOLD, HE IS IN THE DESERT; GO NOT FORTH: BEHOLD, HE IS IN THE SECRET CHAMBERS; BELIEVE IT NOT. Verse 27: FOR AS THE LIGHTNING COMETH OUT OF THE EAST AND SHINETH EVEN UNTO THE WEST; SO SHALL ALSO THE COMING OF THE SON OF MAN BE. Verse 28: FOR WHERESOEVER THE CARCUSES IS, THERE WILL THE EAGLES BE GATHERED TOGETHER. Verse 29: IMMEDIATELY **AFTER** THE TRIBULATION OF THOSE DAYS SHALL THE SUN BE DARKENED, AND THE MOON SHALL NOT GIVE HER LIGHT, AND THE STARS SHALL FALL FROM HEAVEN, AND THE POWERS OF THE HEAVENS SHALL BE SHAKEN. Verse 30: AND THEN SHALL APPEAR THE SIGN OF THE SON OF MAN IN HEAVEN: AND THEN SHALL ALL THE TRIBES OF THE EARTH MORN, AND THEY SHALL SEE THE SON OF MAN COMING IN THE CLOUDS OF HEAVEN WITH POWER AND GREAT GLORY'.

Please note that while the Lord Jesus runs down these unpleasant future events, He never once said to his disciples: Do not fear these things for while they are happening on earth, you'll be safe in heaven with Me. Or, you'll only see these things from afar, but they will not happen to you. Nor, 'Thousands shall fall on your right hand and tens of thousands on your left, but it shall not come nigh thee'.

Apocalyptic Catastrophies

There are many other catastrophes in peoples apocalyptic thinking that are not mentioned in **Matthew chapter 24** by the Lord Jesus at all. These include the leftist propaganda about global warming caused by the emission of greenhouse gases resulting in the so called flooding of the world's coastal regions.

Every morning I have to go from my house on the mainland side of Daytona Beach, Florida across a bridge to City Island Library. I must go to the City Island Library as I don't have my own computer to write this book on and must use their timed public one. (Their public computer is timed for use at only two hours per day per patron).

The bridge that I must cross was built back in 1962 when I was young and used to play in the water beneath it as it was being built. I have first hand personal experience then to know that the level of the water has not changed since then. So this unsubstantiated and twisted mindset that because of global warming Florida will be flooded is just not true, not for Daytona Beach anyway.

There is however a problem with global warming that no one wants to recognize. That is the oceans are getting warmer and some ice is melting because way off the coast of Peru underwater volcanic eruptions and geothermal venting are occurring across a wide section of the South Pacific. By these deep cold water of the South Pacific is being heated up significantly at over 700 degrees Fahrenheit. Then this hot water enters ocean currents that push it around the world so far as to even melt the glaciers in the arctic regions. Thus global warming is not being caused by hydrocarbon pollution resulting from the burning of fossil fuels. This Socialist Propaganda and delusionary stupidity is being adopted by the anti-capitalist socialists who have absorbed this delusional misdiagnosis from the environmentally insane.

There are other problems caused by government experimentation with weather modification. One of these involves using contrails sprayed from the air to supposedly seed the clouds with metal particles to reduce global warming but actually cause 'global diming'. 'Global diming' is actually reducing the sun's rays by 20% resulting in plants that won't grow and soil contamination from metal particles (aluminum).

Those of you surviving where hurricane Sandy hit are aware that something seems to be wrong with the weather.

As a person who has experienced numerous hurricanes in Florida, I know by experience that most hurricanes that skirt the east coast of America eventually turn out to sea. Such is normal as hurricanes desire warm water much more than the obstructions of land. Therefore it appears obvious that some form of weather modification directed this hurricane to turn left to hit the Northeast instead of going out to sea.

The United States government is experimenting with weather modification and weather weapons to be used in war. This program was called HAARP. Unfortunately, in order to perfect such weapons experimentation on the civilian population is required.

Most non-Christians could not accept this truth. But it is no coincidence that this hurricane tore up several blue states who voted for anti-God political pollution including abortion, gay marriage and socialism to force workers to support bums. Later in this book when I discuss the best places to relocate to I'll be sure to mention: **Avoid living in any blue states or states that are turning blue at all costs, for our God still judges sin and those who support sin.**

I'll probably have to move from my home in Florida where I grew up some day because all these Northerners who like our sunny weather bring down with them their liberal, ant-God political pollution. Most Northerners are nominal Catholic. And they vote for anti-God, pro abortion, and gay rights candidates. This hypocrisy demands judgment and for my own welfare I must avoid it by moving away.

There are other unfortunate events that the Lord Jesus did not mention as being a part of 'the beginnings of sorrows' listed in Matthew 24 including the valid but overemphasized concern over the possibility of a major volcanic eruption on land. It is possible that Yellowstone could erupt and bury America under a mountain of volcanic ash. If that should happen, you'd have no choice but to move out of its way, if you could. For Yellowstone is a super volcano whose eruption is now overdue. Super means that its big caldera (its large pool of molten rock) is over twenty square miles big. That means that this volcano contains not just cubic yards of magma but cubic miles of this contaminate. Such can inundate the entire nation all the way to the Atlantic Ocean and Gulf of Mexico.

Back in 1969 when Apollo landed on the moon, an environmental photo of the surrounding area showed that the moon was a desert wasteland as far as the eye can see. If Yellowstone were to erupt all of America, East, North and South of Yellowstone, Wyoming would be covered with lava, pumas and volcanic ash to the boarders and to the sea. That means that the only states to be spared the original blast of the eruption might include Alaska, Hawaii, California, Oregon, Washington, Idaho, Nevada and Arizona. Every other state would be buried under lava, pumas and volcanic ash all the way to the Atlantic Ocean and Gulf of Mexico.

Such a catastrophe would also pollute the air worldwide and turn summer into winter, as in nuclear winter. It would be so massive an event that it would blot out the sun world wide for at least 2 years. That means that all crops would fail worldwide. And those people living in Europe would not be able to see to do anything like even to get to work.

Worldwide commerce would end. There would be no more access to any ports on the East Coast and Gulf Coast of America. The New York Stock Exchange, the Chicago Mercantile Exchange and Midwest Bread Basket would be no more. For all practical purposes, life as we have known it in America will have ended.

I hear someone crying after this happens: 'How could God have allowed such a thing to happen?' To them I say: **'Be not deceived God is not mocked whatsoever a man sows that shall he also reap......they that sow to the flesh shall of the flesh reap destruction' (Galatians 6:7).**

Because our God is longsuffering, patient and loving this may not happen in your lifetime but remember that according to the Geological record it's now overdue. Anyway here is a lesser tragedy that the Lord Jesus never mentioned but will come your way some day.

The Canary Islands owned by Spain and off the Coast of Africa in the Atlantic Ocean have a couple of volcanoes too. If just one of them erupts it could split that island in half, resulting in a massive landslide into the Atlantic Ocean. This could generate a title wave high enough to strike the entire East Coast of America. This title wave would then push mountains of sea water inland at least 20 miles and so cause great loss of life.

Because title waves are not like regular waves at the seashore which moves in cycles or wave links. Whereas a title wave just keeps coming. In other words; when a regular wave hits you at the beach it may knock you off your feet at first, but then it quickly goes back out to sea and gives you enough time to catch your breath. But a title wave knocks you down and keeps you down as it just keeps coming. It does not give you a chance to catch your breath so that you drown.

Moreover just the regular waves during 'the beginnings of sorrows' will be roaring **(Luke 21:25) 'And there shall be signs in the sun, and in the moon, and in the stars; and upon the earth the distress of nations; with perplexity; the sea and the waves roaring'.**

These fearful sights and great signs from heaven also include the possible astronomical hazard of a meteor **(Luke 21:11)** or asteroid impact that the Lord Jesus does not mention as being in **the beginnings of sorrows of Matthew 24.** But this catastrophe is listed in other scriptures **(Luke 21: 11 and Mark 20:13)** that the Lord Jesus did say. We know that eventually these things will happen for they are described in the book of Revelation. But just because this chapter of **Matthew 24** does say that the stars will fall from heaven, does not mean that they're gonna fall on you.

I guess the 'troubles' coming in **Mark 13:8** as being part of 'the beginnings of sorrows' could include every nature of catastrophe and every manor of calamity including: poll shift, collisions with planets, asteroids, comets and meteors, solar storms, EMP attack, social unrest, economic turmoil resulting from economic depression and resulting race riots of the unemployed, bird flu epidemics, AIDS and EBOLA pandemics, volcanic eruptions with resource depletion resulting from overpopulation causing despots to deprive people of both basic human and their God given rights.

The sun and moon were also given in your Bible **(Genesis 1:14)** as signs to indicate what's coming. The ancient scribes said that changes in the moon referred to coming changes with Israel as the book entitled: Four Blood Moons by John Hagee depicts. It appears that Israel's national future is about to change for the better. **It's going to win some future wars to expand its borders to those of the covenant that God made with Abraham.**

During this time of four consecutive blood moons occurring on Jewish Feast days happens to fall a total solar eclipse right in the middle of those Blood Moons on March 20, 2015. **This may be very significant since a total solar eclipse at this time of Blood Moons on feast days indicates God's judgments upon the nations for every nation and people group that has ever come against Israel, especially those that have tried to force Israel to give up its covenant land for peace.**

Any nation, like America which forces Israel to divide its land for a Palestinian state may just find its own land divided by God in an earthquake.

Another part of this judgment will be war as Israel will be given the opportunity to reconquer that Promised Land again to update Israel's claim on that land. I hope then that Israel will do what Joshua did when he took Jericho. Remember from the fall of America that diversity (many gods) and pluralistic democracy (many committees) does not please God. 'For God so loved the world that He did not send us a committee'. The commandment: 'Thou shalt have no other Gods before Me' is still the word of God! Those who will not honor and worship the God of Israel must vacate His land!

My Economy

In addition to these two already mentioned I also have two more rather unpleasant situations that the Lord Jesus never mentioned in Matthew 24 but will make our lives in these end times very uncomfortable. The first one has to do with the economy. First to encourage you I'll give my recent experience with this. Several years ago as this same financial crisis was going from bad to worse I happened to be watching the Inspiration Network on TV in which David Cerullo of (InspirationCampmeeting.com 1-888-488-1377) had as his guest Mike Murdock (the famous prosperity teacher). Brother Mike told us about his conversation with Oral Roberts. In which he told us that he asked Oral: 'what was the most important thing that God ever gave you?' Oral answered right away, without even taking time to think it over and said: 'seed faith'.

God gave Oral the idea of seed faith in order to raise money so that he could build O.R.U. for the people of God. In other words, Oral Roberts had a prophetic vision about his university first, and then God gave him the idea of seed faith in order to raise sufficient funds to bring his vision into manifestation.

After sharing this history, Brother Mike went on to authenticate the practice of 'seed faith' as the legitimate method of raising funds that God has supposedly given to all ministers and ministries.

OBJECTION: Oral Roberts is one individual man of God, not the entire New Testament Church, nor is what God gave him to fulfill his vision apply to all ministers (some of whom are just fly by night pseudo-evangelists who need to get a real job and stop begging the people of God to support them).

In Florida many retirees are being ripped off by internet gamblers masquerading as charities. These con artist gamblers seduce the elderly to send them 'seed money' to secure their lotto or sweepstakes winnings. Of course then their 'seed money' is just confiscated by this rip-off scam.

In this light, it does not seem wise to me to be raising money by this rip-off method of 'seed faith' when such a scheme is the common scam used by internet gamblers to rip-off and defraud the elderly.

Before I go on I hear other objections to Brother Mike and the prosperity message. It is probably well known that Brother Mike has now become wealthy and lives in an exclusive, large, luxury, home in Fort Worth, Texas. So luxurious that when tourists come to town they take helicopter rides to see the city of Fort Worth from the air. They also make a pass over Brother Mike's home to show it off as in Hollywood, California they also show off the fabulous homes of the famous movie stars.

Mike Murdock's dad who also lives with Brother Mike was once a pastor back in the old days when Christian church members believed that low income would keep a Pastor humble. So Brother Mike grew up in some parsonages that a chicken coop could put to shame.

Some feel that brother Mike's desire for luxurious accommodations now is sinful, but the truth is that his current desire is a psychological compensation to make up for the lack of adequate housing during his childhood.

Just today when I took the kid shopping at Wal-Mart we went down the road that is parallel to the flight path of airplanes here in Daytona Beach. We noticed that many private jets were flying into Daytona Beach airport every few minutes from all over the country for the Daytona 500 NASCAR RACE.

Some socialists say that these expensive planes (the toys of multimillionaires) need to be confiscated for things like expanded Head Start, expanded Medicaid and unlimited unemployment compensation. In other words share the wealth by redistributing it.

Look, as the Bible says and as I see it: financial wealth is a gift from God, not something to be seized by some liberal or socialist government so that a bunch of lowlife thugs can trample it underfoot.

It does no good to expand Head Start if it's just going to result in more educated criminals. What good does it do to expand Medicaid so that those infected with AIDS and EBOLA can now recover and get strong enough to infect more innocent people. And if people remain unemployed for too long they'll forget how to do those tasks that can earn them 'a descent livable wage'.

So I am not jealous of what Brother Mike has. Nor am I gonna waste my life praying, fasting and begging God to get what he has. Luxury homes just don't 'turn me on' and luxury is not my thing anyway. I'd rather do exploits for God.

If I need prosperity I don't have to give 'love' offerings to some prosperity preacher anyway. All I need to do is to pray for the peace of Jerusalem as the Bible says; 'they shall prosper that love thee' (Psalm 122:6). I hope this answers your objections as I need to move on to share more previously suppressed truth.

Personally, I'd rather expand my anointing more than to increase my prosperity anyway. I remember when Katharine Khulman would pass by people and they would fall 'slain in the Spirit'. When she lived in Pittsburg, Pennsylvania and had to go to the airport there to make her flight for her meetings. As she passed by the people to get in line and board her flight, people would fall out 'under the power'. So much so that the airport authorities gave her a special pass to use the underground service tunnel (Used to put meals on planes) so that she could get on her plane and the others could get on theirs and go too.

But there is a higher anointing than that which I'd like to have. This has already happened right here in America once before. Early in the last century a man, one of the Pentecostal pioneers of the faith, had gone to hold evangelical meetings in the liberal haven of San Francisco. His name was Smith Wigglesworth. This man was so anointed that the locals of San Francisco used to put their sick folk on sickbeds outside by the sidewalk so that when Smith Wigglesworth passed by to go to his meetings his shadow might fall on the sick and heal them.

As I see it, that's a wonderful way to do real ministry. No preaching was required (that would be good for me, since I have a speech impediment due to a head injury). And no offering was taken up. When you do God's work, God pays you Himself and I'd rather receive Spiritual gifts like this than even gold coins.

Later in that same TV Show Brother David Cerullo offered a blessing pack for ten dollars to support both his TV Ministry and for us to get the stuff that we wanted from God. I wasn't very excited about getting something from God, as I didn't need very much back then. So I got up to change the channel, thinking that what Brother Mike Murdock had shared with us was all that I needed back then. But just then Brother David Cerullo showed us what was in his blessing pack. My eyes immediately saw beyond a few trinkets and tokens to a Mezuzah.

One summer when I was a kid we had to leave Daytona Beach because my dad worked on a yacht that had to move down to Miami. While there we lived next door to a wealthy Jewish family. They had a son about my same age back then that I used to play with. He also taught me some Hebrew that I still remember.

One day I asked him about this Mezuzah I saw high up in the entrance door of his family's home. He told me that that device was put there to bless the home back when the house was brand new and before his family moved in. Remembering this, that that Mezuzah had to go with a new home, I quickly gave my ten dollars for that blessing pack offered by Brother David Cerullo's Inspiration Ministry. When that blessing pack came I kept only the Mezuzah and threw the other tokens and trinkets away. I then took that Mezuzah and put it away in my safe and forgot about it.

I do not consider myself to be a particularly holy man. I didn't have a bunch of severe problems to pray about back then, nor needs to beg God for and I still don't believe in giving to get and thus manipulating God. The only reason that I sent in my ten dollars was because I knew from childhood that that Mezuzah had to go with a new home and with it I'd be better prepared and ready to receive from God my new home. But I didn't put any demands on God nor beat Him over the head with his Word to get what I wanted. As I learned from the Presbyterians at Fuller Seminary; <u>God is Sovereign that means He can do what He wants, when He wants, anyway He wants. What's undeserved is on Him. You don't demand blessings from a Sovereign. You thank Him for whatever comes.</u>

You guessed it, this is an open rebuke of 'the blab it and grab it, name it and claim it' crowd. With God you don't insist or demand. Though you are a child of God you do not act like children. For **'when I became a man I put away childish things'.** Its manipulating children who like to tell their parents: 'Mommy you said this' or 'Daddy you said that'. Circumstances may have changed now; Daddy may have lost his job. Mom's car may have broken down and now she needs all the money that she can get in order to fix it. Well God is the God of the universe. So, I'm sure that He has other concerns that take priority over your measly problems of wanting something just to outshine the Jones's or just to confirm your beliefs about prosperity. **'Be content with such things as you have' (Hebrews 13:5). And (Philippians 4:11) 'I have learned, in whatsoever state I am, therewith to be content'. 'But Godliness with contentment is great gain' (I Timothy 6:6).**

Anyway here's what happened: in May of that year it rained bad and flooded out some including me in my neighborhood. The governor declared this part of Florida a disaster area. Part of a big tree, limbs and all, crashed through my roof and got the inside of my house wet. So I applied for assistance. Of course there was a bureaucratic mix up and one agency gave my request to another. But in time, the inspectors came to inspect my damage. They almost tripped coming into my old house as the floors were warped from that rain. Then they saw this old dump that me and the kid were living in. The walls in the kitchen where the roof fell in were covered with mold. They were horrified and I remember that they asked the kid: 'Aren't you guys ever sick?' The kid said; 'No we're Christians. We don't get sick, we're always blessed'.

The inspectors ignored that and looked around some more and saw a big hole in the kitchen floor, its warped door, its broken cabinets, its hazardous electric wiring and other extensive damage and so wrote on the report the word: '**replacement**'. Then we were called down to the City Hall where the city officials said that we have been approved by HUD for the replacement of our home. So we had to move out while our new house was being built up to code. I was surprised as the new building code required reinforced concrete construction with a hurricane proof roof.

Anyway all of this happened while millions of people were out of work, millions of foreclosed homes were sitting around empty, some couldn't even get enough food to eat and millions of those same foreclosed homes had driven many families into homelessness. While I was blessed far beyond my imagination I still can't figure it all out. All I know is that I exercised my token faith to believe that Mezuzah would be on my new home.

I'm only sharing this now to encourage those of you who maybe encountering very difficult economic times right now. From all indications this economy will get worse but you can still overcome as the Jimmy Swaggert Singers sing that our anchor will hold despite the coming storm.

Brother David Cerullo of the Inspiration Network has a famous dad, the Prophet Morris Cerullo who has a New Economic Bible that you can purchase for $59 at (Morris Cerullo World Evangelism). It discloses not just how to prosper but also how to survive in these last days.

Another famous modern prophet also a Messianic Jew, Rabbi Jonathon Cahn told us in his first book entitled: The Harbinger that judgments would be coming our way if we fail to repent. Since we failed to repent after 9 11 the 2001 financial judgment came. Then also the one of 2008 came too.

Rabbi Jonathon Cahn tells us in his new book entitled: <u>The Mystery of The Shemitah </u>on page 228 just how this same financial judgment could happen again. Both of the two previous Shemitah cycles of 2001 and 2008 ended or climaxed in the greatest stock market crashes in history. So this next Shemitah cycle may do likewise. Especially since America has not repented from turning away from God. Moreover if everything comes in 3's and judgments increase and intensify after the solar eclipse of March 20, 2015 the same financial judgment could happen again toward the end of this Shemitah year which runs from September 2014 to September 2015. **Therefore 9/11/ 2015 is a very bad day for the economy. But then the second solar eclipse of 2015 which happens on September 13, 2015, the day of nullification of the Shemitah year will come to be known as the day of shaking signaling America's fall.**

Individual Wealth Transfer

Another part of your economic condition that the Lord Jesus Christ does not mention in **Matthew 24** has to do with wealth transfers and Christians becoming rich before going to heaven. The prosperity people say that this is primarily because of the need to have wealth to fund the end time harvest.

While the Bible does mention that **'seed time and harvest will not end as long as the earth remains' (Genesis 8:22).** This particular scripture refers to agriculture (farming) and not mass production evangelism necessitating technology to get out the gospel message. Like television and satellite dishes, engineering, air and cable time and satellite rent. It does not mention Christian's need to have wealth to fund the end time harvest of souls via color television programs with paid actors, satellite dishes, internet or expensive smart phones connected to some mission base in America.

'Money answers all things' (Ecclesiastes 10:19) and according to the prosperity people, there have been supposedly 3 major wealth transfers listed in the Bible. I intend to cover them all for you here. First I want to deal with the first individual wealth transfer involving Abraham.

His was the first Biblically recorded and divinely sanctioned wealth transfer of an individual. Note how that we are not told about Abraham's position in life. Neither how holy he was nor how educated and spiritually gifted he may have been. This first example of individual wealth transfer does not define Abraham but affirms the sovereignty of his God instead.

Sovereignty is a word some Christians mistakenly delegate to the theology of Calvinism with all its hyper-election opposed to one's free will. But we are not discussing theology here but the majesty of God showing forth his right and prerogative to do what he wants anyway he wants. So let's read Genesis chapter 12.

'Now the Lord said to Abram, Get thee out of thy country, and from thy kindred, and from thy father's house, unto a land that

I will show thee: And I will make of thee a great nation, and I will bless thee, and make thy name great; and thou shalt be a blessing; And I will bless them that bless thee, and curse him that curseth thee; and in thee shall all the families of the earth be blessed. So Abram departed, as the Lord has spoken unto him; and Lot went with him; and Abram was seventy and five years old when he departed out of Haran. And Abram took Sarai his wife, and Lot his brother's son, and all their substance that they had gathered, and the souls that had gotten in Haran; and they went forth to go into the land of Canaan; and into the land of Canaan they came. And Abram passed through the land unto the place of Sicham, unto the plain of Moreh. And the Canaanite was then in the land. And the Lord appeared unto Abram, and said, **Unto thy seed will I give this land**; and there builded he an altar unto the Lord, who appeared to him. And he removed from thence unto a mountain on the East of Bethel, and pitched his tent, having Bethel on the west, and Hai on the east: and there he built an alter unto the lord, and called upon the name of the Lord. And Abram journeyed, going on still toward the South **(Genesis 12:1-9)**.

'The earth is the Lord's' (Psalm 24:1) and as the Sovereign of all creation it's God's right and prerogative to give any part of it to whomever He will. As Sovereign, He is the owner deciding how it is to be parceled outand to whom, not the Canaanites, or in modern times, not the Palestinians. **At once this clearly shows from scripture that the two state solution for Palestine is error. All the land there belongs to Abraham's seed which goes through Isaac and then Israel.**

The second wealth transfer of an individual also involves Abram when he experienced great famine in Canaan and went down into Egypt. This story is recorded in your Bible **(Genesis 12:10-20)**.

'And there was a famine in the land; and Abram went down into Egypt to sojourn there; for then famine was grievous in the land. And it came to pass, when he was coming near to enter into Egypt, that he said to Sarai his wife, Behold now, I know that though art a fair woman to look upon; Therefore it shall come to pass, when the Egyptians shall see thee, that they shall say, This is his wife; and they will kill me, but they will save thee alive. Say, I pray thee, thou art my sister; that it may be well with me for thy sake: and my soul shall live because of thee. And it came to pass, that, when Abram was come into Egypt, the Egyptians beheld the woman that she was very fair. The princes also of Pharaoh saw her, and commend her before Pharaoh, and the woman was taken into Pharaoh's house. And he entreated Abram well for her sake: and he had sheep, and oxen, and asses, and menservants, and maid servants, and she asses, and camels. And the Lord plagued Pharaoh and his house with great plagues because of Sarai Abram's wife. And Pharaoh called Abram, and said, What is this that thou hast done unto me? Why didn't thou not tell me that she was thy wife? Why saidest thou, She is my sister? So I might have taken her to me to wife; now therefore behold thy wife, take her, and go thy way. And Pharaoh commanded his men concerning him; and they sent him away, and his wife, and all that he had' **(Genesis 12:10-20).**

These verses bring out that Abram felt that he had to engage in misrepresentation by inducing Sarai his wife to lie that she was Abram's sister instead. I suppose that the Dutch also had the need to lie to the Nazis about the Jews they were hiding. Note should be made here that even though moral values were violated still God blessed. In that light, Pharaoh, a mere heathen, respected Abram's wife more than some modern American pastors who marry divorced people and now even gays so Pharaoh and Egypt were blessed back then.

When Pharaoh recognizes Abram's sin of lying and possibly defrauding him, he nevertheless refused to take Sarai for himself but forced out both Abram and his wife. The Pharaoh, thou heathen, nevertheless refused to play get back for Abram's lying and let him leave with all his stuff, unlike most Christians he did not require Abram to pay for his sin and give back the stuff that Pharaoh gave him.

This section of scripture brings out a few more truths which will offend some people. The first is democracy.

I once heard a joke that said: 'For God so loved the world that he did not give us a committee'. In that light it should be obvious that no committee of any political party established to govern has ever been anointed by God to rule. But kings and queens as sovereigns have been anointed to rule. I'm sure that you all have heard of 'The divine right of kings'.

In this case, the Pharaoh was the sovereign ruler of Egypt. As such, God could deal with him personally even though he was a heathen. And that's just what He did. Somehow the Spirit of Truth revealed to him that Abram had lied to him about Sarai being his sister instead of being his wife.

As the sovereign over Egypt, it was a Pharaoh's right to overrule moral convention and take Sarai to himself to wife anyway. But sovereigns over nations usually respect for their own good the Sovereign of the universe, especially where curses and plagues are concerned. So that Pharaoh must have thought just from common sense that the best way to get rid of any curse or plague was to get rid of those behind it. So he had both Abram and Sarai put out of Egypt with all their stuff. **So this was not really a wealth transfer as such**, but rather an eviction from the peace, prosperity and safety of Egypt out to the desert where nothing grows. Of course God still took care of them both (Abram and Sarai). Continued to bless them and returned them to Canaan in spite of Abram's sin.

Pharaoh was still a wealthy man. So his wealth was not transferred to Abram. God just used Pharaoh to bless Abram despite his naughtiness. That's the kind of blessing we'd all like to have.

It is true that Pharaoh lavished gifts such as sheep, oxen, camels, donkeys and servants upon Abram because of Sarai.

But it is NOT true that God took the wealth of Pharaoh away from him and gave it to Abram. Thou Abram had much stuff and left Egypt with great herds of all kinds of livestock, servants, gold and silver **(Genesis 13:2). Pharaoh remained undiminished. Still in power, still wealthy and still secure as the sovereign of Egypt. So no real wealth transfer happened here.** Instead Abram was blessed despite his sin just like most Christians today.

Now Abram was very rich **(Genesis 13:2)**, and so also was Lot **(Genesis 13:5)**. So much so that the land could not bear them both **(Genesis 13:6).**

So they separated and Lot chose the plain of Jordan **(Genesis 13:11).** While Abram dwelled in the land of Canaan **(Genesis 13:12).**

Lot encountered wars which ripped him off **(Genesis chapter 14).** But Abram rescued him **(Genesis 14:16).** And paid tithes to Melchizedek **(Genesis 14:20). Here we do see the wealth transfer of the wicked kings who abused Lot was transferred to Abram by conquest in war (called spoils). So this real transfer of wealth involved bloodshed.**

The prosperity people now have us turn to **Genesis 26:1-14** to see their next transfer of wealth.

'And there was a famine in the land, beside the first famine that was in the days of Abraham. And Isaac went into Abimelech king of the Philistines unto Gerar. And the Lord appeared unto him, and said, Go not down into Egypt; dwell in the land which I shall tell thee of; Sojourn in this land, and I will be with thee, and will bless thee; **for unto thee, and unto thy seed, I will give all these countries, and I will perform the oath which I swear unto Abraham thy father.** And I will make thy seed to multiply as the stars of heaven, **and will give unto thy seed all these countries;** and in thy seed shall all the nations of the earth be blessed; Because that Abraham obeyed my voice, and kept my charge, my commandments, my statutes, and my laws.

And Isaac dwelt in Gerar. And the men of the place asked him of his wife; and he said, She is my sister: for he feared to say, She is my wife; lest, said he, the men of the place should kill me for Rebekah: because she was fair to look upon. And it came to pass, when he had been there a long time, then Abimelech king of the Philistines looked out at a window, and saw, and, behold, Isaac was sporting with Rebekah his wife. And Abimelech called Isaac, and said, Behold, she is thy wife; and how saddest thou, She is my sister? And Isaac said unto him, Because I said, Lest I die for her. And Abimelech said, What is this thou hast done unto us? One of the people might lightly have lain with thy wife, and thou shouldest have brought guiltiness upon us. And Abimelech charged all his people, saying, He that touches this man or his wife shall surely be put to death. Then Isaac sowed in that land, and received in the same year an hundred fold; and the Lord blessed him. And the man waxed great, and went forward, and grew until he became very great. For he had possession of flocks, and possession of herds, and great store of servants: and the Philistines envied him' **(Genesis 26:1-14).**

In verse three, God tells Isaac that He will bless him. Then in verse five God tells him why (because Abraham his father obeyed God's voice, statutes, commandments and laws). (In modern times we see the son of Jimmy Swaggart blessed because of his father's obedience too). Isaac was also told in verse three that his seed will inherit all these countries. But then in verse seven we see him repeating what Abraham did in calling his wife his sister in order to stay alive himself. But by so doing he could have brought sin upon Abimelech's people. Abimelech found out that Rebekah was really Isaac's wife when he saw Isaac caressing her **(Genesis 26:8).** Then Abimelech confronted Isaac in order to keep his men free from sin.

The ancients felt that marriage was to be held in high honor. And both parties to the marriage were held immune to all sexual advances. So in verse eleven: 'Abimelech charged all his people, saying; He that toucheth this man or his wife shall surely be put to death'.

But single people in the ancient world were free to have sex. The ancient world was loaded with prostitutes, both male and female. Many prostitutes were servants of various false gods and those having sex with them were keeping up their devotional life by doing so. In other words, having sex was a part of a young unmarried person's worship and devotion to some false god.

After this marriage and sex issue was settled back then it says in verse twelve: 'Then Isaac sowed in that land, and received in the same year an hundred fold; and the Lord blessed him'. Then in verse thirteen it goes on to say: 'And the man waxed great and went forward, and grew until he became very great'. Then verse fourteen says: 'He had possession of flocks, and possession of herds, and great store servants; and the Philistines envied him'.

At no point in these few verses does it ever say that the wealth of Abimelech was transferred to Isaac.

As a student there (at Fuller Theological Seminary) I participated in chapel service every week with the other students. Although it was held in a Presbyterian Church, its service was opened to all students of all denominations therefore I felt free to prophesy to 'the body of Christ' there and did so. Back then I was also receiving truths from the Holy Spirit including this one:

The last individual wealth transfer that these prosperity people put forth is recorded in **Genesis 31:1-9**. Now let's look at that:

'And he heard the words of Laban's sons, saying, Jacob hath taken away all that was our father's; and that which was our father's hath he gotten all this glory. And Jacob beheld the countenance of Laban, and, behold, it was not toward him as before. And the Lord said unto Jacob. Return unto the land of thy fathers, and to thy kindred; and I will be with thee. And Jacob sent and called Rachel and Leah to the field unto his flock. And said unto them. I see your father's countenance, that it is not toward me as before; but the God of my father hath been with me. And ye know that with all my power I have served your father. And your father hath deceived me, and changed my wages 10 times; but God suffered him not to hurt me. If he said thus, The speckled shall be thy wages, then all the cattle bare speckled; and if he said thus, The ring straked shall be thy hire; then bear all the cattle ring straked. Thus God hath taken away the cattle of your father, and given them to me' (Genesis 31:1-9).

As you can see in verse 9 above, God took away the cattle of Laban and gave them to Jacob. **This is the clearest example of a genuine individual wealth transfer that I see in the word of God.** Things like this can happen and may happen before Jesus comes again especially if you know how to involve God in your problems, to obtain the favor of God and to merit the blessings of God by obedience to His word.

I particularly like this Biblically recorded incident because it shows that our God (the God of Israel) is not just a lovey, dovey, esoteric, divine nature God but as the God of Israel He also has some Jewish qualities as well. Here He out deals the dealer or out cons the conman just like any New York Jew. Laban was determined to screw Jacob over his pay, so God screwed Laban instead. This is the kind of real justice that we need to see more of today.

If you go to lawyers about your problems especially with other Christians however you're just supposed to suffer yourselves to be defrauded **(I Corinthians 6:7).** This of course is the solution to personal problems like domestic disputes that the pacifists like most. But if you let God handle your problems His way, He will do so, but you may not like the result.

I remember that after I graduated from Fuller Seminary and could not find a job due to my wheelchair disability. Since 'wheelchairs do not inspire faith'; and I could no longer live in that college's dorms and could not afford the high rents out there in Southern California so I wound up living out on the streets with the homeless. I adopted part of their lifestyle to raise money for my personal needs and to re-give to some worthwhile ministries, so I begged at the local shopping center. That night after begging all day, I laid down with the homeless. But about 3:00am a local cop kicked me awake and wrote me a citation for trespassing on his city's land.

I didn't argue with that cop. After he left I remembered from Bible study that when the king of Israel received a threatening letter from the king of Syria, he laid it before the Lord. So I threw down my citation before God and told Him that this cop said that I was trespassing on his city's land. But the word of God says in **Psalm 24** that **'the earth is the Lord's'**. So I wouldn't be paying any fine or doing any time as I was 'more sinned against than sinning' and have done nothing wrong. Then I told God that I was tired, was going back to sleep and He could handle this any way He saw fit.

The next morning I went by bus to the mission to eat my oatmeal. As we went by the local police station, I saw that their flag was flying at half-staff.

Once I arrived at the mission, I asked the mission director what had happened. He told me that I could read all about it in his morning paper which I could take with me after I ate.

After I ate, I grabbed the paper and caught the bus to the shopping center where I worked (begging back then).

Since the cars didn't start coming through till the stores opened at 10:00am and I arrived at 9:30am, I had time to read that article. It was a very sad story about how this policeman had shot himself to death in a fire arms accident that happened at the same time when I gave my citation matter to God for Him to handle His way.

Then the article proceeded to read like an obituary complete with family photos and one of that policeman graduating from the police academy. Further on that article gave the policeman's full name. Of course I looked for my citation to compare the name the cop had signed on it with the full name in the article. They matched.

I was devastated and felt that to take someone's life just over trespassing was overkill. He was a nice looking young man and had a family too. But I remembered right away what I had learned from the men of God at Fuller Seminary: ' whenever you ask God to intervene into your problems and tell Him that He's free to do whatever he wants, don't dare complain about whatever He does, don't dare tell Him that his action was an overreaction, too much or too harsh. **You don't correct God.** Accept whatever He does. You don't need to understand it. Remember God's ways are past finding out, so don't try to figure things out. Thank Him and move on'.

Now I hear the pacifists saying in considering this issue. That one should **'submit yourselves to every ordinance of man' (I Peter 2:13).** But where would America be today if our ancestors had obeyed the English Tea Tax? <u>In this situation, I didn't think of this verse or Romans 13 but of Psalm 24 as the real issue in this case was about land and who owned it.</u> This shows the clear value of being baptized in the Holy Ghost and studying God's word so that you may **'rightly divide the word of truth' (II Timothy 3:15).**

National Wealth Transfer? Joseph

We already covered the clearest example of a genuine individual wealth transfer that I see in the word of God. This individual wealth transfer involved Laban from whom that wills in the form of cattle went to Jacob the father of Joseph. Jacob of course was favored by God who would not allow Laban to screw him out of his wages. In fact, God intervened to assure Jacob's payment at Laban's cost.

You've heard the old idiom, 'like father, like son'. That's what we have here. The following case with Joseph is supposedly the most significant national wealth transfer in the word of God.

Joseph was used by God to exercise his spiritual gift (the interpretation of dreams) to rescue an entire heathen nation plus the people of God. **This is the best example of a national wealth transfer in which everyone was blessed.** This account concerning Joseph exists in your Bible. But since some of you may have forgotten it from Sunday School, I'll now share it with you:

'Now Israel (Jacob) loved Joseph more than all his children, because Joseph was the son of his old age: and he made him a coat of many colors. And when his brethren saw that their father loved him more than all his brethren, they hated him, and could not speak peaceably unto him. And Joseph dreamed a dream and he told it to his brethren and they hated him yet the more. And he said unto them, Hear, I pray you, this dream which I have dreamed: For, behold, we were binding sheaves in the field, and, lo, my sheaf arose, and also stood upright; and, behold, your sheaves stood round about, and made obeisance to my sheaf, and his brethren said to him, Shalt thou indeed reign over us? Or shalt thou indeed have dominion over us? And they hated him yet the more for his dreams, and for his words' **(Genesis 37:3-8).**

'And he dreamed yet another dream, and told it to his brethren, and said, Behold, I have dreamed a dream more; and, behold, the sun and the moon and the eleven stars made obeisance to me. And he told it to his father, and to his brethren: and his father rebuked him, and said unto him, what is this dream that thou has dreamed? Shall I and thy mother and thy brethren indeed come to bow down ourselves to the earth? And his brethren envied him; but his father observed the same' **(Genesis 37: 9-11).**

This short portion of scripture tells us a few things which any reputable Sunday school would bring out. First, wise marriage and family councilors say that parents should not favor one child above others as this is the naughty act of favoritism which results first in resentment and then in revenge.

Second: where a naughty act exists, a spiritual atmosphere does not. That's why Joseph's brothers could sell him into slavery.

Third: if you're a spiritual person with God's gift of dreaming spiritual dreams, you don't share the spiritual with the everyday or mundane.

Fourth: if you're dreams evidence the gift of prophecy, find someone spiritual like your pastor to share them with. It's important to let others that are spiritual both judge and confirm your gift **(I Corinthians 2:15 and 1:8).**

Fifth: **'since all that live godly in Christ Jesus shall suffer persecution' (II Timothy 3:12),** expect others to resent your gifting and to feel the need to bring you down to earth.

If Joseph was the favorite in his household then he probably received the major share of that family's spiritual resources. In any case, someone took the time to help make Joseph into a holy and pure person. Since such would be necessary to operate in the prophetic gifts. (This is noted in the last sentence of **Genesis 37:11** where it says that his father observed the sayings).

In time Joseph found himself tempted by an unscrupulous woman. Unfortunately most of us have been used, abused, and misused too.

This situation went from bad to worse as the woman lied to her husband about Joseph's supposed rape of her, so Joseph was sent to prison.

'But the Lord was with Joseph, and showed him mercy, and gave him favor in the sight of the keeper of the prison. And the keeper of the prison committed to Joseph's hand all the prisoners that were in the prison; and whatsoever they did there, he was the doer of it. The keeper of the prison looked not on anything that was under his hand; because the Lord was with him, and that which he did, the Lord made it prosper' **(Genesis 39:20-23).**

But in prison Joseph continued interpreting dreams: 'And it came to pass after these things, that the butler of the king of Egypt and his baker had offended their lord the king of Egypt, And Pharaoh was wroth against two of his officers, against the chief of the butlers, and against the chief of the bakers, And he put them in ward in the house of the captain of the guard, into the prison, the place where Joseph was bound. And the captain of the guard charged Joseph with them, and he served them: and they continued a season in ward. And they dreamed a dream both of them, each man his dream in one night, each man according to the interpretation of his dream, the butler and the baker of the king of Egypt, which were bound in the prison' **(Genesis 40:1-5).**

'And Joseph came in unto them in the morning, and looked upon them, and, behold, they were sad. And he asked Pharaoh's officers that were with him in the ward of his lord's house, saying, wherefore look ye so sadly today? And they said unto him, we have dreamed a dream, and there is no interpreter of it. And Joseph said unto them, do not interpretations belong to God? Tell me them, I pray you' **(Genesis 40:6-8).**

'And the chief butler told his dream to Joseph, and said to him, In my dream, behold, a vine was before me; And in the vine were three branches; and it was as though it budded, and her blossoms shot forth; and the clusters thereof brought forth ripe grapes: And Pharaoh's cup was in my hand; and I took the grapes, and pressed them into Pharaoh's cup, and gave the cup into Pharaoh's hand. And Joseph said unto him, this is the interpretation of it: the three branches are three days: Yet within three days shall Pharaoh lift up thine head, and restore thee unto thy place: and thou shall deliver Pharaoh's cup into his hand, after the former manner when thou wast his butler. But think on me when it shall be well with thee, and show kindness, I pray thee, unto me, and make mention of me unto Pharaoh, and bring me out of this house: For indeed I was stolen away out of the land of the Hebrews: and here also I have done nothing that they should put me into the dungeon' **(Genesis 40:9-15).**

'When the chief baker saw that the interpretation was good, he said unto Joseph, I also was in my dream, and, behold, I had three white baskets on my head: And in the uttermost basket there was of all manner of bake meats for Pharaoh; and the birds did eat them out of the basket upon my head. And Joseph answered and said, This is the interpretation thereof: The three baskets are three days: yet within three days shall Pharaoh lift up thy head from off thee, and shall hang thee on a tree; and the birds shall eat thy flesh from off thee. And it came to pass the third day, which was Pharaoh's birthday that he made a feast and all his servants: and lifted up the head of the chief butler and of the chief baker among the servants. And he restored the chief butler unto his butlership again: and he gave the cup into Pharaoh's hand: But he hanged the chief baker; as Joseph had interpreted to them. Yet did not the chief butler remember Joseph, but forgot him': **(Genesis 40:16-23).**

As you can see, Joseph spake the truth to the chief baker even though it was negative. It's usually unwise to give any negative information from a prophetic spiritual gift especially to an unspiritual person. But as all evangelists know both the positive and negative charges must be presented to create the spark of power resulting in Holy Ghost revival.

But before we move on we should mention one fact for you that are concerned about nutrition and better personal health: Notice in verse 17 that the baker fed Pharaoh all manner of 'bake meats'. In other words meats covered with real whole wheat bread (not like today's genetically modified synthetic bread). Then these were baked in an oven. Not fried in fattening grease.

But far more important is the fact that Joseph continued to exercise his spiritual gift 'no matter what'. This set Joseph up to be used by God to 'save much people alive' despite the famine that was coming.

Although the chief butler forgot Joseph, God would give Joseph another chance to exercise his spiritual gift and this time even on a higher level since Joseph had shown himself to be faithful.

This next time the Pharaoh of Egypt had a dream: 'And after two full years, Pharaoh dreamed that he stood by the river (Nile). And, behold, there came up out of the river seven well-favored kine and fat fleshed; and they fed in a meadow. And, behold, seven other kine came up after them out of the river, ill favored and lean fleshed; and stood by the other kine upon the bank of the river. And the ill favored and lean fleshed kine did eat up the seven well-favored fat kine. So Pharaoh awake. And he slept and dreamed the second time: and, behold, seven ears of corn came up upon one stalk, rank and good. And, behold, seven thin ears blasted with the east wind spring up after them. And the seven thin ears devoured the seven rank and full ears. And Pharaoh awoke, and, behold, it was a dream. And it came to pass in the morning that his spirit was troubled; and he sent and called for all the magicians of Egypt, and all the wise men thereof: and Pharaoh told them his dream; but there was none that could interpret them unto Pharaoh. Then spake the chief butler unto Pharaoh, saying, I do remember my faults this day: Pharaoh was wroth with his servants, and put me in ward in the captain of the guard's house, both me and the chief baker. And we dreamed a dream in one night, I and he; we dreamed each man according to the interpretation of his dream. And there was with us a young man, an Hebrew, servant of the captain of the guard: and we told him, and he interpreted to us our dreams; to each man according to his dream he did interpret. And it came to pass, **as he interpreted to us, so it was: me he restored to mine office, and him he hanged**. Then Pharaoh sent and called Joseph, and they brought him hastily out of the dungeon and **he shaved himself, and changed his raiment**, and came in unto Pharaoh. And Pharaoh said unto Joseph, I have dreamed a dream, and there is none that can interpret it and I have heard say of thee, that thou canst understand a dream to interpret it. And Joseph answered Pharaoh, saying, it is not in me: God shall give Pharaoh an answer of peace. And Pharaoh said unto Joseph, In my dream, behold, I stood upon the bank of the river: And, behold, there came up out of the river seven kine, fat fleshed and well-favored; and they fed in a meadow: And, behold, seven other kine came up after them, poor and very ill favored and lean fleshed, such as I never saw in all the land of Egypt for badness. And the lean and the ill favored kine did eat up the first seven fat kine: And when they had eaten them up it could not be known that they had eaten them: but they were still ill favored, as at the beginning. So I awoke. And I saw in my dream, and, behold, seven ears came up in one stalk, full and good: And, behold, seven ears, withered, thin, and blasted with the East wind, sprang up after them: And the thin ears devoured the good ears: and I told this unto the magicians; but there was none that could declare it to me. And Joseph said unto Pharaoh, The dream Pharaoh is one: **'God has shown Pharaoh what he is about to do' (Genesis 41:1-26).**

The chief butler gave his testimony to Pharaoh that Joseph's spiritual gift of interpreting dreams was truthful in predicting the actual outcome of his and the chief baker's dreams. Thus the dreams were prophetic and everyone knew it. So this motivated Pharaoh to call for Joseph to interpret his prophetic dream also.

Personal hygiene is rarely mentioned in any Bible school today, since the spiritual is not always practical. In the days of Jesus men did not use deodorant nor brush their teeth. Of course Jesus and his disciples opponents probably felt that like all common men back then their doctrines also 'stank to high heaven'.

Notice that Joseph had the common sense, decency and proper decorum (not just his spiritual gift) to shave himself and to also change his clothes before he went before Pharaoh (as recorded in underlined verse 14 above).

Today I know of many pastors who have their own breath mints that they take both before the service and after it when they are interacting with people. While the Bible does not say that 'cleanliness is next to godliness', nevertheless you can't be filthy if you want to lead people into cleanliness of both the body and the spirit. You especially don't want to offend people with bad breath (halitosis) or body odor when you're trying to get them reconciled to God and prayed through. Deadly bad breathe does not help to regenerate one to the New Birth.

Then Joseph began his interpretation by saying that: 'The seven good kine are seven years; and the seven good ears are seven years: the dream is one. And the seven thin and ill favored kine that came up after them are seven years: and the seven empty ears blasted with the east wind shall be seven years of famine. This is the one thing which I have spoken unto Pharaoh: **What God is about to do he showeth unto Pharaoh.** Behold, there comes seven years of great plenty throughout all the land of Egypt. And there shall arise after them seven years of famine; and all the plenty shall be forgotten in the land of Egypt; and famine shall consume the land; And the plenty shall not be known in the land by reason of that famine following; for it shall be very grievous. And for that the dream was doubled unto Pharaoh twice: it is because the thing is established by God, and God shall surely bring it to pass'. **(Genesis 41:26-32).**

Since I also interpret prophetic dreams as part of my ministry there are a few points in here that need to be emphasized for your understanding: First, I underlined what Joseph said to Pharaoh about what God was showing him. It's important to let people know that they are being used by God and trusted with information that could benefit both them and the people that they serve. In other words they are being used as a partner in this thing with God.

Notice in verse 32 that Joseph makes mention that this dream was doubled. Whenever a dream is given in two different forms or with two different subjects that means that the dream is a Prophetic dream and as such it is certain and its interpretation is sure. Like real prophecy it will happen. You can count on it.

'Now therefore let Pharaoh look out a man discrete and wise, and set him over the land of Egypt. Let Pharaoh do this, and let him appoint officers over the land, and take up the fifth part of the land of Egypt in the seven plenteous years. And let them gather all the food of those good years that come, and lay up corn under the hand of Pharaoh, and let them keep food in the cities. And that food shall be for store to the land against the seven years of famine, which shall be in the land of Egypt: that the land parish not through the famine' **(Genesis 41:33-36).**

To look for a man discrete and wise to do this is understandable. But one filled with the Holy Ghost and wisdom obviously takes precedence. That's probably why Pharaoh chose Joseph to do this task for him and his nation.

To appoint officers shows wisdom in sharing the task with others.

To keep the food in the cities means it will be watched over and kept safe.

To keep it under the hand of Pharaoh means that God wants to use Pharaoh's assistant to do this task and they must have the highest authority in the land in order to make Pharaoh's God sent prophetic dream a reality.

The basic reason or theme behind the dream is clearly expressed publically. The Pharaoh is told by Joseph as he gives his interpretation and solution that the purpose is that God wants Pharaoh to rescue and save the land of Egypt from the coming famine.

'And the thing was good in the eyes of Pharaoh, and in the eyes of all his servants. And Pharaoh said unto his servants, Can we find such a one as this is, a man in whom **the Spirit of God is?** And Pharaoh said unto Joseph, forasmuch as God has shown thee all this, there is none so discrete and wise as thou art. Thou shalt be over my house, and according unto thy word shall all my people be ruled: only in the thrown will I be greater than thou. And Pharaoh said unto those people, See, I have set thee over all the land of Egypt. And Pharaoh took off his ring from his hand, and put it up on Joseph's hand, and arrayed him in vestures of fine linen, and put a gold chain about his neck: and he made him ride in the second chariot which he had; and they cried before him, Bow the knee; and made him ruler over all the land of Egypt. And Pharaoh said unto Joseph, I am Pharaoh, and without thee shall no man lift up his hand or foot in all the land of Egypt. And Pharaoh called Joseph's name Zaphnach-paaneah; and gave him to wife Asenath the daughter of Poti-pherah priest of On. And Joseph went out over all the land of Egypt. And Joseph was thirty years old when he stood before Pharaoh King of Egypt. And Joseph went out from the presence of Pharaoh, and went throughout all the land of Egypt'. **(Genesis 41:37-46).**

When the Pharaoh began speaking he made mention that the Spirit of God was in Joseph as I underlined above. When the Spirit of God is in you others recognize it. According to all common precedence someone in whom the Spirit of God is, is higher up the ladder of gifting then an educated man, or an experienced magician or even a clairvoyant or remote viewer.

Even the unsaved, the heathen and the pagan can recognize it when the Spirit of God is in someone. And they want to be near that blessed person so that they might be blessed also as in verse **38 of chapter 41 of Genesis.**

Pharaoh had the common desire of wanting to give back. So recognizing that Joseph was a young man, he gave Joseph Asenath the daughter of the priest of On to wife (This was an arranged marriage which no one could object to).

To some this might seem strange but since Joseph gave forth his spiritual gift to benefit the whole nation of Egypt, the Pharaoh of Egypt had the right to reward Joseph as he saw fit.

This true story about Joseph almost moves me to tears because of its prophetic significance. It also depicts a young man being used by God to bless an entire nation as well as his own people. But the prosperity preachers also use this account of Joseph to authenticate their 'wealth transfer' doctrine.

Some feel that any spiritual gift is exclusively for the people of God and not also for a secular or heathen nation. In this case Joseph's gift was being used by a heathen king to rescue his own ungodly nation from famine. By Joseph's giving of his spiritual gift of interpretation his people, the people of God would also be blessed. **So this was not a real wealth transfer but like the blessing of rain which falls on the just and the unjust (Matthew 5:45).** Now let's look at a real wealth transfer:

Real National Wealth Transfer: Moses

A real 'wealth transfer' is usually like receiving an inheritance. One cannot receive the inheritance until the testator dies. In other words, a real wealth transfer occurs when someone dies that you benefit from or are the beneficiary of just like in an insurance policy.

The greatest example of this is in your Bible when Moses led the children of Israel out of Egypt **(Exodus 3:4-10).** Now let's look at that:

'God said, Do not come near; put your shoes off your feet, for the place on which you stand is Holy Ground. Also He said, I am the God of your father, the God of Abraham, the God of Isaac, and the God of Jacob. And Moses hid his face, for he was afraid to look at God. And the Lord said, I have surely seen the affliction of My people who are in Egypt, and have heard their cry because of their taskmasters and oppressors; for I know their sorrows and sufferings and trails. And I have come down to deliver them out of the hand and power of the Egyptians and to bring them up out of that land to a land good and large, a land flowing with milk and honey (a land of plenty) to the place of the Canaanite, the Hittite, the Amorite, the Perizzite, the Hivite, and the Jebusite. Now behold, the cry of the Israelites has come to Me, and I have also seen how the Egyptians oppress them. Come now therefore, and I will send you to Pharaoh, that ye may bring forth my people, the Israelites, out of Egypt'.

'And Moses said unto God, who am I that I should go unto Pharaoh, and that I should bring forth the children of Israel out of Egypt' **(Exodus 3:11).**

'And He said, Certainly I will be with thee; and this shall be a token unto thee, that I have sent thee: When thou hast brought forth the people out of Egypt, ye shall serve God upon this mountain' **(Exodus 3:12).**

'And Moses said unto God, Behold, when I come unto the children of Israel, and shall say unto them, The God of your fathers hath sent me unto you; and they shall say to me, What is His name? What shall I say unto them? **(Exodus 3:13).**

'And God said unto Moses, I AM THAT I AM: and He said, Thus shall thou say unto the children of Israel, I AM hath sent me unto you' (Exodus 3:14).

Back when I was a boy in the 1950's my parents and I went to see at a drive-in movie depicting what happened next called: The Ten Commandments, staring Charlton Heston as Moses. After a while, as the judgments began to happen I thought I was watching a horror film:

1. The first judgment was about the waters of Egypt becoming blood **(Exodus 7:15-24).**

'Go to Pharaoh in the morning; he will be going out to the water; wait for him by the river's bank; and the rod which was turned into a serpent you shall take in your hand. And thou shalt say unto him, the Lord God of the Hebrews hath sent me unto thee, saying, Let My people go, that they may serve Me in the wilderness; and, behold, hitherto thou wouldest not hear. Thus saith the Lord, in this thou shalt know that I am the Lord; behold, I will smite with the rod that is in my hand upon the waters which are in the river, and they shall be turned to blood. And the fish that is in the river shall die, and the river shall stink; and the Egyptians shall loathe to drink of the water of the river. And the Lord spake unto Moses, Say unto Aaron, Take thy rod, and stretch out thine hand upon the waters of Egypt, upon their streams, upon their rivers and upon their ponds, and upon all their pools of water, that they may become blood; and that there may be blood throughout all the land of Egypt, both in vessels of wood, and in vessels of stone. And Moses and Aaron did so, as the Lord commanded; and he lifted up the rod, and smote the waters that were in the river, in the sight of Pharaoh, and in the sight of his servants; and all the waters that were in the river were turned to blood. And the fish that was in the river died; and the river stank, and the Egyptians could not drink of the water of the river; and there was blood throughout all the land of Egypt. And the magicians of Egypt did so with their enchantments; and Pharaoh's heart was hardened, neither did he harken unto them: as the Lord had said. And Pharaoh turned and went into his house; neither did he set his heart to this also. And all the Egyptians digged round about the river for water to drink: for they could not drink of the water of the river' **(Exodus 7:15-24).**

2. The second judgment was the plague of frogs that also infested the river of Egypt and Egypt's land too **(Exodus 7:25 – Exodus 8:7).**

'And seven days were fulfilled, after that the Lord had smitten the river. And the Lord spake unto Moses, Go unto Pharaoh, and say unto him, Thus saith the Lord, Let My people go, that they may serve Me. And if thou refuse to let them go, behold, I will smite all thy borders with frogs. And the river shall bring forth frogs abundantly, which shall go up and come into thine house, and into thy bedchamber, and upon thy bed, and into the house of thy servants, and upon thy people, and into thine ovens, and into thy kneading troughs; And the frogs shall come up both on thee, and upon thy people, and upon all thy servants. And the Lord spake unto Moses, Say unto Aaron, Stretch forth thine hand with thy rod over the streams, over the rivers, and over the ponds, and cause frogs to come up upon the land of Egypt. And Aaron stretched out his hand over the waters of Egypt; and the frogs came up, and covered the land of Egypt. And the magicians did so with their enchantments, and brought up frogs upon the Land of Egypt' **(Exodus 7:25 thru Exodus 8:7).**

3. The third judgment which the Lord sent upon Egypt was the plague of lice **(Exodus 8:16-19).**

'And the Lord said unto Moses, say unto Aaron, Stretch out thy rod, and smite the dust of the Land, that it may become lice throughout all the land of Egypt. And they did so; for Aaron stretched out his hand with his rod, and smote the dust of the earth, and it became lice in man, and in beast; all the dust of the land became lice throughout all the land of Egypt. And the magicians did so with their enchantments to bring forth lice, but they could not; so there were lice upon man, and upon beast. Then the magicians said unto Pharaoh, **This is the finger of God:** and Pharaoh's heart was hardened, and he harkened not unto them; as the Lord had said' **(Exodus 8:16-19).**

4. The fourth judgment which the Lord sent upon Egypt was the plague of flies **(Exodus 8:20 and 21).**

'And the Lord said unto Moses, Rise up early in the morning, and stand before Pharaoh: lo, he cometh forth to the water; and say unto him, Thus saith the Lord, let My people go, that they may serve Me. Else, if thou wilt not let my people go, behold, I will send swarms of flies upon thee, and upon thy servants, and upon thy people, and into thy houses; and the houses of the Egyptians shall be full of swarms of flies, and also the ground whereon they are' **(Exodus 8:20&21).**

This particular curse should have been significant to the Egyptians because flies are attracted particularly to dead stuff that stinks. So many flies about indicated death. This was certainly not a good sign for Egypt.

5. Sure enough the next curse involved death, the death of Egypt's cattle was plague number 5 **(Exodus 9:1-7).**

'Then the Lord said unto Moses, Go in unto Pharaoh, and tell him, thus saith the Lord God of the Hebrews, Let My people go, that they may serve Me. For if thou refuse to let them go, and wilt hold them still, Behold, the hand of the Lord is upon thy cattle which is in the field, upon the horses, upon the asses, upon the camels, upon the oxen, and upon the sheep: there shall be a very grievous murrain. And the Lord shall sever between the cattle of Israel and the cattle of Egypt; and there shall nothing die of all that is the children's of Israel. And the Lord appointed a set time, saying, tomorrow the Lord shall do this thing in the land. And the Lord did that thing on the morrow, and all the cattle of Egypt died; but the cattle of the children of Israel died not one. And Pharaoh sent, and, behold, there was not one of the cattle of the Israelites dead. And the heart of Pharaoh was hardened, and he did not let the people go' **(Exodus 9:1-7).**

6. The six judgment that God sent upon Egypt was the plague of boils and blains **(Exodus 9:8-12).**

'And the Lord said unto Moses and unto Aaron, Take to you handfuls of ashes of the furnace, and let Moses sprinkle it toward the heaven in the sight of Pharaoh. And it shall become dust in all the land of Egypt, and shall be a boil breaking forth with blains upon man, and upon beast, throughout all the land of Egypt. And they took ashes of the furnace, and stood before Pharaoh; and Moses sprinkled it up toward heaven; and it became a boil breaking forth with blains upon man, and upon beast. And the magicians could not stand before Moses because of the boils; for the boil was upon the magicians, and upon all the Egyptians. And the Lord hardened the heart of Pharaoh, and he harkened not unto them; as the Lord hath spoken unto Moses' **(Exodus 9:8-12).**

Boils in particular usually result from filthy air. Example:-air in modern times which is polluted by coal dust and causes boils in the lungs called 'black lung'. Or pumas or volcanic ash resulting from volcanic eruptions which people breathe in, their lungs explode in boils, and then solidify like cement and they die by suffocation which like drowning is a very unpleasant way to die.

7. The seventh plague that God sent to Egypt was the plague of hail and fire **(Exodus 9:13-26).**

'And the Lord said unto Moses, Rise up early in the morning, and stand before Pharaoh, and say unto him, Thus saith the Lord God of the Hebrews, Let My people go, that they may serve Me. For I will at this time send all My plagues upon thine heart, and upon thy servants, and upon thy people; that thou mayest know that there is none like Me in all the earth. For now I will stretch out My hand, that I may smite thee and thy people with pestilence; and thou shalt be cut off from the earth. And in very deed for this cause have I raised thee up, for to show in thee My power; and let My Name be declared throughout all the earth. As yet exalted thou thyself against My people, that thou wilt not let them go? Behold, tomorrow about this time I will cause it to rain a very grievous hail, such as hath not been in Egypt since the foundation thereof even until now. Send therefore now, and gather thy cattle, and all that thou hast in the field; for upon every man and beast which shall be found in the field, and shall not be brought home, the hail shall come down upon them, and they shall die. He that feared the word of the Lord among the servants of Pharaoh made his servants and his cattle flee into the houses; And he that regarded not the word of the Lord left his servants and his cattle in the field. And the Lord said unto Moses, Stretch forth thine hands toward heaven, that there may be hail in all the land of Egypt, upon man, and upon beast, and upon every herb of the field, throughout all the land of Egypt. And Moses stretched forth his rod toward heaven; and the Lord sent thunder and hail, and the fire ran along upon the ground; and the Lord rained hail upon the land of Egypt. So there was hail, and fire mingled with hail, very grievous, such as there was none like it in all the land of Egypt since it became a nation. And the hail smote throughout all the land of Egypt all that was in the field, both man and beast; and the hail smote every herb of the field, and break every tree of the field. Only in the land of Goshen, where the children of Israel were, was there no hail.

8. The eighth plague that the Lord visited upon Egypt was the plague of locust **(Exodus 10: 1-7).**

'And the Lord said unto Moses, Go in unto Pharaoh; for I have hardened his heart, and the heart of his servants, that I might show these My signs before him: And that thou mayest still in the years of thy son, and of thy son's son, what things I have wrought in Egypt, and my signs which I have done among them; that ye may know that I am the Lord. And Moses and Aaron came in unto Pharaoh, and said unto him, Thus saith the Lord

God of the Hebrews, How long wilt thou refuse to humble thyself before Me? let My people go, that they may serve Me. Else, if thou refuse to let My people go, behold, tomorrow will I bring the locust into thy coast: And they shall cover the face of the earth, that one cannot be able to see the earth: and they shall eat the residue of that which is escaped, which remaineth unto you from the hail, and shall eat every tree which growth for you out of the field: And they shall fill thy house, and the houses of all thy servants, and the houses of all the Egyptians; which neither thy fathers, nor thy fathers' fathers have seen since the day that they were upon the earth unto this day. And he turned himself, and went out from Pharaoh. And Pharaoh's servants said unto him, How long shall this man be a snare unto us, let the men go, that they may serve the Lord their God: **knowest thou not yet that Egypt is destroyed?' (Exodus 10:1-7).**

It seems then that Pharaoh was ready to harken to his servants and he called for Moses and Aaron to come before him again. **Exodus 10:8** confirms this. Pharaoh however asked them the question about who should go, which Moses answered in **Exodus 10:9;**

'And Moses said, We will go with our young and with our old, with our sons and with our daughters, with our flocks and with our herds will we go; for we must hold a feast unto the Lord'. But Pharaoh said: 'Not so; go now ye that are men, and serve the Lord; for that ye did desire. And they were driven out from Pharaoh's presence'. The Lord didn't like this, so He spoke to Moses again saying: 'And the Lord said unto Moses, stretch out thine hand over the land of Egypt for the locust that they may come upon the land of Egypt, and eat every herb of the land, even all that the hail hath left. And Moses stretched forth his rod over the land of Egypt, and the Lord brought an east wind upon the land all that day, and all that night; and when it was morning, the east wind brought the locust. And the locust went up over all the land of Egypt, and rested in all the coasts of Egypt: very grievous were they; before them there were no such locust as they, neither after them shall be such. For they covered the face of the whole earth, so that the land was darkened; and did eat every herb of the land, and all the fruit of the trees which the hail had left; and they remained not any green thing in the trees, or in the herbs of the field, through all the land of Egypt' **(Exodus 10:9-15).**

'Then Pharaoh called for Moses and Aaron in hast; and he said, I have sinned against the Lord your God, and against you. Now therefore forgive, I pray thee, my sin only this once, and entreat the Lord your God, that He may take away from me this death only. And he went out from Pharaoh, and entreated the Lord. And the Lord turned a mighty strong west wind, which took away the locusts, and cast them into the Red sea; there remained not one locust in all the coast of Egypt. But the Lord hardened Pharaoh's heart, So that he would not let the children of Israel go' **(Exodus 10:16-20).** So God sent another plague.

9. The Lord God of the Hebrews sent this ninth plague of darkness.

'And the Lord said unto Moses, Stretch out thine hand toward heaven, that there may be darkness over the land of Egypt, even darkness which may be felt. And Moses stretched forth his hand toward heaven; and there was a thick darkness in all the land of Egypt three days; they saw not one another, neither rose any from his place for three days; but all the children of Israel had light in their dwellings' **(Exodus 10:21-23).**

'And Pharaoh called unto Moses, and said, Go ye, and serve the Lord: only let your flocks and your heards be stayed; and let your little ones also go with you. And Moses said, Thou must give us also sacrifices and burnt offerings, that we may sacrifice unto the Lord our God. Our cattle also shall go with us; there shall not an hoof be left behind; for therefore must we take to serve the Lord our God; and we know not with what we must serve the Lord, until we come thither. But the Lord hardened Pharaoh's heart, and he would not let them go. And Pharaoh said unto him, Get thee from me, take heed to thyself, see my face no more; for in that day thou seest my face thou shalt die. And Moses said, Thou hast spoken well, I will see thy face again no more' **(Exodus 10:24-29).**

10. Now God sent the tenth, or last plague upon Egypt **(Exodus 11:1-10).**

'And the Lord said unto Moses, yet will I bring one plague more upon Pharaoh, and upon Egypt, afterwards he will let you go hence; when he shall let you go, you shall surely thrust you out hence altogether. Speak now in the ears of the people, and let every man borrow of his neighbor, and every woman of her neighbor, jewels of silver, and jewels of gold. And the Lord gave the people **favor** in the sight of the Egyptians. Moreover the man Moses was very great in the land of Egypt, in the sight of Pharaoh's servants, and in the sight of the people. And Moses said, Thus says the Lord, About Midnight will I go out into the midst of Egypt: And all the firstborn in the land of Egypt shall die, from the first born of Pharaoh that sitteth upon his throne, even unto the firstborn of the maidservant that is behind the mill; and all the firstborn of beasts. And there shall be a great cry throughout all the land of Egypt, such as there was none like it, nor shall be like it anymore. But against any of the children of Israel shall not a dog move his tongue, against man or beast; that ye may know how that the Lord doth put a difference between the Egyptians and Israel. And all these thy servants shall come down unto Me, and bow down themselves unto Me, saying, Get thee out, and all the people that follow thee: and after that I will go out. And he went out from Pharaoh in a great anger. And the Lord said unto Moses, Pharaoh shall not harken unto you; that My wonders may be multiplied in the land of Egypt. And Moses and Aaron did all these wonders before Pharaoh: then the Lord hardened Pharaoh's heart, so that he would not let the children of Israel go out of his land'.

There are certain things about these judgments upon Egypt which need to be brought out. No commentator has mentioned that the God of the universe calls Himself the Lord God of the Hebrews in Exodus 9:1, 9:13 and 10:3. Here He brings Himself down from an ethereal Spirit Light Being without human emotions to the human emotion of being a wronged Hebrew that needs to get even by demonstrating His vengeance.

The idealistic pre-tribulation rapture position holds that God will get all Christians out of this earth before any tribulation happens. When tribulations (God's judgments) were brought upon Egypt, the Hebrews were not totally immune from all those judgments.

There is no mention in the first plague visited upon Egypt, where the water became blood, that the land of Goshen where the Hebrews were was spared. In fact in **Exodus verses 19 & 21** it is brought out that this plague of water turned to blood was to be throughout all the land of Egypt apparently including Goshen. Likewise the next plague of frogs came upon all Egypt and their servants **(Exodus 8 verse 4).** The next plague of lice also came upon all men and beasts throughout all the land of Egypt **(Exodus 8 verse 17).**

Then when the plague of flies came it says in verse 22 that there were no flies in the land of Goshen. In the next plague it also says in **Exodus 9:4** that when the death of Egypt's cattle happened nothing died of what belonged to the children of Israel.

But the next plague of boils and blains happened throughout all the land of Egypt **(Exodus 9:9).**

But the plague of hail with fire spared the land of Goshen, where the children of Israel were **(Exodus 9:26).**

Then the plague of locusts which came next covered all the land of Egypt **(Exodus 10:14).**Then came the plague of darkness which also covered all the land of Egypt for three days **(Exodus 10:32).**

Then the last plague came which shows forth a situation that every person should note. This plague involving the death of the first born covered the whole of Egypt, only it did not affect the children of Israel **(Exodus 11:7),** who followed the instructions of the Passover.

From the first judgments upon Egypt apparently including the children of Israel too, it would seem to any logical person that the mid-tribulation rapture theory if congruent to these judgments upon Egypt would be the most correct viewpoint.

But from then on the judgments alternate from Israel being immune, to it being included because they also inhabited the land of Egypt.

The last plague probably brings out the real truth of what this Great Tribulation Rapture will really be like: only those who are covered by the blood of the Lamb (the Lord Jesus Christ) will be spared the total destruction of the Great Tribulation and go on into eternal life yet remain here to witness this great tribulation first hand just like the children of Israel did in Egypt.

It should be noted that our God is a personal God. He wants His people to see what He does for them. So we may be here to see first hand His wrath poured out in the Great Tribulation even though we are not appointed to wrath. Appointment in this case means being the recipient. So we can still witness it but be protected from it. It wouldn't be written, if we were not to witness it first hand, just like the children of Israel did in Egypt.

As recorded below, then the Passover happened in which none of the children of Israel died because God had told them '**when I see the blood, I will pass over you'.**

'And the Lord spake unto Moses and Aaron in the land of Egypt, saying, This month shall be unto you the beginnings of months; it shall be the first month of a year to you. Speak ye unto all the congregation of Israel, saying, In the tenth day of this month they shall take to them every man a lamb according to the house of their fathers, a lamb for an house; And if the household be too little for the lamb, let him and his neighbor next unto his house take it according to the number of souls; everyman according to his eating shall make you count for the lamb. Your lamb shall be without blemish, a male of the first year; ye shall take it out from the sheep, or from the goats. And ye shall keep it up until the fourteenth day of the same month; and the whole assembly of the congregation of Israel shall kill it in the evening. And they shall take of the blood, and strike it on the two side posts and on the upper door post of the houses, wherein they shall eat it. And they shall eat the flesh in the night, roast with fire, and unleavened bread; and with bitter herbs they shall eat it. Eat not of it raw, nor sodden at all with water, but roast with fire; his head with his legs, and with the pertinence thereof. And ye shall let nothing of it remain until morning; and that which remaineth of it until the morning ye shall burn with fire. And thus shall ye eat it, with your loins guarded, your shoes on your feet, and your staff in your hand; and ye shall eat it in hast: it is the Lord's Passover. For I will pass through the land of Egypt this night, and will smite all the first born in the land of Egypt, both man and beast; and against all the god's of Egypt I will execute judgment; I am the Lord. And the blood shall be to you for a token upon the houses where you are; and when I see the blood, I will pass over you, and the plague shall not be upon you to destroy you, when I smite the land of Egypt' **(Exodus 12:1-13).**

We have just read about the Passover. Although it is widely felt that a Christian minister, who is also a prophetic person should dissect and examine every part of this passage. I will not play ministerial monopoly by doing so. Since the Passover is a national heritage of the Jews. I'll let the completed, messianic Jews of South Florida who went to Hebrew school and understand the Hebrew language discuss the meanings of the Passover's various symbols themselves.

As a Christian leader this Passover to me boils down to just one word. That's what prophetic people do: take what is complicated and make it into a simple truth that's easy to understand. **That word is 'blood'**. The Lord said: 'when **I see the blood, I will pass over you'**. In Bethel Tabernacle years ago we used to sing that song back in the days of the Jesus Movement, when we all knew by first hand personal experience 'The power of the blood of the Lamb'.

Most of us 'born again' Christians still believe '**that without the shedding of blood there is no remission' for sins (Hebrews 9:22).** And that '**we have redemption through His blood' (Ephesians 1:7 & Colossians 1:14).**

We Christians believe as the Lord Jesus said in **Mathew 26:28 'For this is My blood of the New Testament, which is shed for many for the remission of sins'. 'For even Christ our Passover is sacrificed for us' (I Corinthians 5:7b).**

Remember that in these last days the Lamb of God (the Lord Jesus) has now become the Lion of the tribe of Judah. Because He humbled himself and became obedient to death, even the death of the Cross, therefore, God has highly exalted Him and given Him a name which is above every name, that at the name of Jesus every knee shall bow of things in heaven and things in earth and things under the earth and that every tongue should confess that Jesus Christ is Lord, to the glory of God the Father (Philippians 2:8-11).

From the Passover, I must also bring out one more point that God wants said as it concerns your future and you probably won't get this message unless I say it. From the Passover Feast a prayer is usually made in Hebrew. That prayer translated into English says: <u>'Blessed be the Lord our God, (King) God of the universe'.</u> To me this indicates that we serve a very big God. So big that it takes the whole universe to contain His majesty!

Evangelist Jimmy Swaggart says that his grandmother used to tell him at her prayer meetings to ask big, since we serve a big God.

Catholic Storm

Let's begin to examine in detail the response or answer the Lord Jesus gave to His disciples in **Matthew 24. In verse 5** the Lord Jesus seems to mainly be concerned about deception and that many false Christs will impersonate Him thereby deceiving many. This confirms what I've already said about extra terrestrial aliens and illegal aliens who will be leading us to worship them.

Many shall indeed be deceived as to what being a real Christian is or is not. The Evangelist Jimmy Swaggart (www.JSM.org 1-800-288-8350) has a good handle on this as his ministry exposes religious cults that are not totally Christian. I've got and you can also get two books that he has published about this: Catholicism and Christianity and The Modern Babylon.

My gifting experience as a Christian Prophetic Minister also enables me to tell the difference between a real Christian and a 'wolf in sheep's clothing', like the Muslim Obama. But besides my gifting you also need solid Biblically based knowledge. So whenever you can get valuable Christian books, please do so.

Before I go on to share some more unpleasant truth confirmed by these other two prophetic books about extra terrestrial aliens; Petrus Romanus and Exo Vaticana by Cris Putnam and Thomas Horn, I'll first share some needed truth about the Roman Catholic Church that concerns their so called problem with pedophile priests.

After I graduated from Fuller Seminary which was the only Seminary in the country with a graduate school of psychology where I took some psychology classes too, I went on to another graduate school in California. I earned there my community college counseling credential and had to take numerous psychology classes in order to do so. In some of those psychology classes I also encountered some future lawyers among other student professionals in training.

Their law school had several courses in law which brought out the true devious nature of the legal profession. I remember how that one of these classes was entitled: 'twisting the truth' and another one was about how to stretch the meaning of words in the English language beyond their real meaning to validate your legal position.

Take for example if you were to have an auto accident in most states you would not be allowed to know whether or not the person that hit you had auto-insurance.

In fact in most trails in Court a hearing of discovery is held to determine just what evidence will be presented in Court. So many juries either convict or dismiss the accused without the benefit of having heard the whole truth in that case.

I once heard a very unpleasant joke about the reason why judges wear black robes. Because black robes are the attire of witches in covens.

Knowing this I would say up front that the Roman Catholic Church has more of a legal problem with con artist lawyers more determined to rip off than solving any real or imagined sexual problems with pedophile priests.

It's not fair to rip off the widow's mite given to church in good faith to pay for these unscrupulous lawyers to live a lavish lifestyle at the church's expense.

There is another spiritual problem here. It is the adopted passive lifestyle of many churches where everything that happens is God's will so people refuse to fight against evil especially when it is clothed in legal garb (robes) with police power. This holds true for eventually accepting the antichrist too.

Moreover instead of covering up these pedophile priests by transferring them to another parish, they should have been defrocked and excommunicated.

Most Protestant Christians may not believe in Catholic doctrine at all. But if one still believes in the Catholic doctrine of transubstantiation, priests must be free of any sin especially sexual sins in order to have the anointing required to do that rite of the church. So many priests have so much sin that they are not now able to convert wine into the blood of Christ in the Eucharist. So much so that now the Catholic Church has a rehab house for alcoholic priests in Michigan.

But those priests whose sins also became criminal should have been prosecuted. The idea of making the whole church pay for any individual's sexual sin is outrageous and anti-American.

The Bible talks about brother going to law with brother before unbelievers about things that pertain to this life and how that by doing so, you do wrong and defraud the church of God **(I Corinthians 6:4-8).**

'Things of this life' include sex. For there is no sex in heaven. As you know, the Bible teaches that in the resurrection they neither marry nor are given in marriage but are as the angels of God in heaven **(Matthew 22:30).** So the Muslim idea of having 73 virgin sex partners for killing a Christian or a Jew in Jihad is false.

Speaking of pedophiles in religion it should be noted that historical evidence shows that the so called prophet Mohamed's wives included a nine year old girl. Isn't that also included in the definition of pedophilia? (Sex with children)

As a person who has taken many psychology classes, I also know about 'learned helplessness'. These so called victims of sexual abuse even and especially if what they say is true, need to get over this and stop allowing it to mentally block them from living out their lives and achieving their life goals by being all they can be in Christ. An example of one over-comer of this is seen over TV every day. You might even know her name, Joyce Meyer.org (1-800-727-9673). Who despite child abuse has now grown up to be a mighty woman of God.

One more event happened in my life which helps to exonerate the Roman Catholic Church. After I graduated from the seminary and from the grad school, I found out that my extensive education was to no avail due to discrimination because of my wheelchair disability.

Since I was in a wheelchair and 'Wheelchairs do not inspire faith', I decided to turn my disability deficit into an asset by begging. When people (donors) saw me in my wheelchair and realized that my disability was real, they gave.

At first, I only begged during the week at various shopping centers to cars with their occupants. In time I progressed to begging outside various churches too because I learned that the people of God were the best givers. I also learned by experience that most Christians gave according to the correctness of their theology. **If they believed that God so loved the world that He gave (John 3:16), then they would give too.**

Back in the early days of me being homeless, I lived with the other homeless in the Civic Center of downtown Santa Ana, California. There our best non Christian givers were the local Buddhists who fed us oriental food on Thursday nights. These people did not try to proselytize anyone or give us a bunch of junk to study about their god. Their food service to us was mainly their community social service. They were very friendly, smiled a lot but did not talk much to anyone. They did not pray but sang and gave us food to eat.

Other groups, mainly Christian gave us food and clothes too. These Christian groups ranged from the Orientals of the Korean Presbyterians to the Jesus People of the main Calvary Chapel in Costa Mesa, California. Only no Black Christian groups ever came to our aid there. (Not everyone cares for the mostly white homeless).

These Jesus People of Calvary Chapel gave us the most there at The Civic Center. I remember that when they gave on weekend nights it took them over half an hour just to set up. They had portable restaurant stoves, and big restaurant pots to cook us all the spaghetti we could eat. They also had many desert donations of all sorts of goodies. They also had professional music groups of artists who sang their songs for us while we ate.

Their service was a night of celebration just like an old fashioned revival. They had prayer teams to pray for individuals, to get them reconciled to God. And they had prophetic teams to get people ready to face their future. Their ministry was wonderful and I never heard any complaints about them. Souls were saved, the sick were healed, marriages were restored, the unemployed found jobs, the Lord Jesus was lifted up plus we got fed a good hot meal to boot. And they gave us all kinds of clothes. Plus in the winter they gave us wool blankets.

Other groups that you would expect some social service ministry from never showed up at all. I guess their theology prevented such outreach. These groups not only included the more established pseudo Christian cults like the Mormons and Jehovah's Witness but also the modern New Age groups like Scientology, Transcendental Meditation, Krishna Consciousness and the Aryan, Black, Asian and Muslim Brotherhoods. Of course no wealthy Muslim groups having all that oil money ever gave us a dime.

Once I moved out of the Civic Center to live on the streets and traveled around more I learned by experience that **the Roman Catholics believing this basic truth (that God so loved the world that He gave, John 3:16) also gave to me too.** My most profitable venture (where I received the most) was at Our Lady Queen of Angels, Roman Catholic Church in Newport Beach, California.

My cheapest experience, where self centered church people assaulted me was at that mega church in Lake Forest, California whose pastor wrote that book about The Purpose Driven Life. It so drove them, that they drove me away in my wheelchair empty.

I learned good theology lessons out on those streets; that gifts and giving reflects one's true relationship to God. But some people are good givers despite the fact that their churches teach some stupid doctrines of men. Even though they may be deceived over all their religious propaganda, they still give from their heart and show God's love. Often one's character as a Christian is exemplified by giving that they are a partaker of the divine nature and members in good standing of the family of God since they evidence the deeds of the Lord Jesus Christ.

Moreover later as a minister of the Maranatha House here in Daytona Beach, Florida, I was often invited to minister at several Charismatic Catholic prayer groups. I was never asked by them to help pray someone out of purgatory. Most Charismatic Catholics see through false doctrine themselves and do not need to be beaten over the head with the King James Bible. So I don't try to do the Holy Ghost's job. They automatically corrected themselves and eventually formed their own churches in the community that still ministers today.

I remember that several of their pastors now were my old friends that I used to surf with at the beach years ago before I became disabled. Back then we were all into nature but now we are all into God. Thank you, Jesus.

I said all that to show you that I am not anti Catholic, but have this truth to impart to my Catholic friends:

On April 17, 2013 the Christian prophet, John Paul Jackson shared over the Jim Baker show that five storms were coming upon America and that this first storm would be religious.

I must further impart to you that this first storm will be Roman Catholic. I already know that this will disappoint some. For they feel as I do that any religious storm must somehow involve the false religion of Islam. But Islam is not a religion at all but a political ideology, like facism of conquest, conversion by the sword.

This religious storm begins with the Catholic prophecy about the succession of Popes given by Saint Malachy. According to this Catholic prophecy this current Pope, Francis I will be the last Pope before God's judgment. Although this Pope is an Argentine, he is of Italian (Roman) descent.

Therefore this Pope fits in perfectly as 'Peter the Roman'. For that's his title as Pope and also his heritage. He also happens to be the first Jesuit Pope.

The Jesuits have been investigating so called extra terrestrial life from their Mount Graham observatory in Arizona. The Vatican official in charge of all this research is Father Consolmagno. He says that: 'All contemporary societies will look to the aliens as the saviors of mankind'.

Vatican astronomer, Father Tanzalla-Nitti also says that: 'A re-reading of the Gospel will have to be conducted once the religious content originating from outside the earth has been verified'.

OBJECTION: If man is created in the image of God (Genesis 1:26) then that image cannot be of extra terrestrial grey dwarfs with big eyes like some goon seen in horror films.

This false teaching about extra terrestrial grey aliens coming to save humanity comes from the top of the Roman Catholic Church down. This is not a grass roots teaching discovered by one of the faithful. Therefore since it is a perversion of God's word once given to man, it must be political propaganda dispensed upon the people to get us to give up our own identity and accept these illegal Latino immigrants and intermarry with them too in order to look just like these 'divine' extra terrestrial grey dwarfs (White + Black + Mexican = grey dwarf). (Mexicans are short, non-white Indians).

Take note however that these so called extra terrestrials will actually be demons with full demonic supernatural power far beyond what man has ever had. And no man can stop them but by confessing the name of Jesus. Therefore quickly become a real born again Christian by faith alone and learn to say: <u>'The Lord rebuke you Satan in the name of Jesus'</u>.

This is very important for the name of the Lord Jesus Christ has awesome power because of his blood which was shed for your sins. Therefore confess that name especially if you encounter any situations you don't understand. **THAT NAME IS A WEAPON** that acts like a grenade or bomb to explode away these demons into fairy dust (these opponents of Christianity will not just be Muslims or liberation theology socialists but demons that are supernaturally armed). So learn to use **THAT NAME NOW**. Get fully prepared for what is coming!

Obama Deception

During the Arab Spring when many dictatorships were falling across North Africa, the Liberals said that such was the long awaited expansion of democracy. But in reality it turned out to be the expansion of The Muslim Brotherhood instead with the support and help of the Obama Administration.

Jimmy Swaggart was one of the few Christian Ministers who said back then that Obama was a Muslim sympathizer. And Michael Savage called Obama 'the Islamic sympathizer in chief' on page 200 of his book: Trickle Down Tyranny. And Obama is really a nominal Muslim by birth and not a Christian at all. There is no Record that Obama was ever baptized Christian in any Christian Church. So Obama is an undocumented phony Christian just like all these illegal aliens are undocumented false Americans. (No baptism certificate – no Christian, no birth certificate – no American).

On page 40 of his book: The Amateur, when Edward Klein asked Dr. Jeremiah Wright, Obama's former racist pastor, if Obama was ever converted from Islam to Christianity. Dr. Wright said: 'That's hard to tell'. Look, if you're saved, you know it, and so does everybody else that's close to you!

Obama's personal hypocrisy reminds me of an incident that happened when I was a child. We called a simple young girl that lived by us Reba residue. Since one day she went home crying to her mother with her face smeared with dog residue. Her simple mother hollered; 'pew, due, residue!'

Then she asked Reba what had happened. Reba said that she found what she thought was chocolate in a neighbor's front yard. Since she was friends with that neighbor's dog she thought that dog wouldn't mind if she ate what she saw that dog drop. But when she picked up what she thought was chocolate it had melted in the sun and ran down her arm and somehow got smeared on her face and then it changed from being chocolate to something that stunk.

Her upset Mother told her to come in right away and take a bath. Well, the child was hurting. So she couldn't say I'm gonna wash your mouth out with soap.

This reminds me of exactly what Obama's election has produced. Here was a man that many Blacks believed was somehow good, sweet, educated, well spoken and chocolate just like them too. But in reality this man turned out to be just something a dog had dropped as his repugnant socialist policies now stunk to high heaven.

For example, when Obama first took office Black unemployment was over 15% but he still had the Congress waste a whole year on his socialist Obamacare. So that at the start of his second term Black unemployment was now up over 19%. In all this time he has taken over all healthcare, student loans, the auto industry and mortgages in an attempt to change capitalism into socialism by promoting his Obamacare at your expense and also vetoing the Keystone Pipeline to keep you from working and busting Social Security with disability for bums.

If Obamacare was so great then how come Democratic Senators and Congressman grant the reward of exemption to Obamacare for those businesses that make political contributions to the Democratic Party?

And all you Christian Denominations who provide social services including hospitals MUST provide sexual services including abortions to your employees under Obama Care while Muslims remain exempt to Obama Care.

Speaking again of Obama Care, there is one issue that has not yet been mentioned. That is Obama Care provides for extended life support services for deformed minority babies (particularly those of illegal aliens and Blacks) who will now grow up to become future socialist voters. That your taxes will support since they will never be able to work just like all those illegal alien children.

Social Work Counselors and Ministers who will become Hospital Chaplains are now being trained to council families to pull the plug on granny in order to save Social Security for these deformed minority babies.

How stupid this racist policy is. Yes Obamacare hurts the elderly and gives false hope to the deformed. The deformed can't amount to much in life unless they encounter Christian healing. So it also seems dumb to have kicked prayer out of school when such will be necessary for these deformed students to succeed in life. If these people have a right to a public education, than that education has a duty to expose them to whatever Christian gifts like healing that may be available to them in this life

The Muslim Obama has also stood by as millions of Americans; both White and Black were unfairly driven out of their homes and into homelessness. For those who somehow may still have homes, Obama has given seventy five million of your tax dollars to help GE build smart electric meters that aid burglars in spying on who's home and what electric appliances you have as they 'case' your house.

Speaking of spying, it is now being done at your expense. Your tax dollars are paying for the Utah Data Center of the National Security Agency (NSA). This agency keeps a record of every phone call and internet transaction that you make. And you are not getting your tax money's worth for there is no evidence that their efforts have ever prevented any terrorist attack. For example, where were they when the Boston marathon bombing happened?

This spying is the main enterprise of the 'military, industrial complex' that former president Eisenhower resented. Back in history several of his advisors (those who also wanted him to appoint that liberal Earl Warren) wanted him to move away from relying upon Christian Prophecy to a more secular and industrial spying on the Soviet Union during the cold war. At that time he used to visit a Christian Prophet in Pasadena California each month to find out what was happening. This worked out well because 'The eyes of the Lord are in every place beholding the evil and the good' (Proverbs 15:3).

But even so this prophetic spying was replaced with expensive 'military industrial' spying that your tax dollars now pay for. Think of all the billions wasted on spy satellites that you could have used. **A country cannot use Christian methods if it's no longer Christian. So it's time for revival.** It's far better to restore prayer and Bible reading to school and make America Christian again than to have to pay excessive taxes to fund expensive drug rehab with other welfare programs and social services that distribute 'free' condoms and birth control pills at your expense.

If real revival is to happen first this fatalistic notion of 'learned helplessness' that all things are supposed to get worse and worse and then the Antichrist will take over this country must be overcome. Several years ago the then President George H.W. Bush (Bush 41) said that America was going to become part of the One World Order. About that same time the famous Bible teacher, Marilyn Hickey said on page 52 of her book: <u>Armageddon</u> that the future Antichrist's world empire would include 'only that part of the world that was once part of the Roman Empire'. So NOT America.

This brings up the misconception that president Obama is secretly the Antichrist. President Obama might have the spirit of Antichrist but he is not that person. The two forerunners of the Antichrist, Napoleon and Hitler were both Europeans. The coming Antichrist will also be a European. But some prophetic scholars say that the Antichrist might be an American or Syrian or some other Muslim. The scriptures however do describe the Beast that will become the Antichrist as coming from out of the sea **(Revelation 13:1).** This proves that he does not come from America,

Revelation 13:2 says that he will have a mouth as a lion. Lion is the symbol for the United Kingdom (England). So he will be able to speak English in great swelling words and blasphemies. Most Europeans can speak English and many European languages too. Islamic people however can speak mainly their native tongue. Example Arabs speak only Arabic.

In **Revelation 13:7** we see that war is coming as the Antichrist will be able to make war with the saints and to overcome them and power was given him over all kindreds, and tongues, and nations. Jimmy Swaggart's Expositors Study Bible says 'this doesn't include the entirety of the world, but rather the area over which he has control, which is basically the area of the old Roman empire'.

So Marilyn Hickey and Jimmy Swaggart, both Spirit filled ministers see the same boundaries to the Antichrist's Empire.

If you remember how that Obama promised change from the Bush policies of Middle East War, Guantanamo terrorist imprisonment, using drones to kill civilians and torturing terrorists.

Here is what has really been happening despite Obama's polished rhetoric: the Middle East war in Afghanistan is continuing and now the one in Syria is due to expand. Guantanamo Bay which holds terrorists beyond the reach of America's constitutional law protections remains opened and still in service. The Obama Administration has used a drone to kill an American citizen. And the Obama Administration's ambassador to Libya and several other Americans were killed by Jihadist Muslims because of resentment over Libya being used as a liberated place to now torture terrorists.

It is now seen to be more advantageous to violate the constitutional, civil and human rights of American Citizens than to throw out the extreme liberal policy of an idealistic pluralistic society complete with Jihadist Muslims (enemies of the people) living among us as mandated by law. Which law is now supreme, the Constitution and freedom of association, or immigration rights with its liberal notion about pluralistic democracy that curses our land?

Moreover, the Muslim Obama is not really an Afro-American Christian as many Blacks believe but a Black African Muslim, descendant from those same Black African Muslims that got rich by selling their Black brothers into slavery.

So the Muslim Obama comes from a Muslim family and was raised as a Muslim. When he went to school every day he had to pray to the false Muslim god, Allah. Most of his schooling during the formative years of childhood took place in the Muslim country of Indonesia.

Speaking of Indonesia it should be noted that the government of that Muslim nation wanting to bless its own people with healing and deliverance among other miracles recently invited in a famous Christian miracle worker who also used to minister here in Florida. (This was done because as Muslims know their Allah is remote, distant and unconcerned about peoples everyday needs).

Indonesia's action may seem strange but such is typical of Muslim nations that really care for the welfare of their people. Those in authority over such nations know that prayers to Allah do not obtain personal blessings for their people. But Jesus whom they consider a mere prophet can both heal and deliver. Though Muslim theology is wrong, God (the God of Abraham) still blesses through Jesus.

In fact what constitutes most Christian prayer is for God to bless people physically, socially and financially. But Muslim prayer (like Obama learned) is for vengeance (Sheria Law), 'social justice' (reclaiming Iraq and Syria for Isis), armaments (like nuclear weapons for Iran) and empowerment to fight and behead the enemies of Islam and to accept martyrdom if need be.

Speaking of Muslim prayer it is also obvious that the child Obama prayed against US forces in Vietnam just like other Muslim students right there in Indonesia. But these prayers didn't seem to work much then. So most Christians would say that this is because the Muslim god Allah is not real but false.

But prayers to a false god cause people to get worked up with the intention to make their prayers come to pass themselves (self fulfilling prophecy). Psychologists say that's what we have here with the Muslim Obama. **(Since Allah can't, Obama will!)** And now subconsciously Obama has cut back America's armaments to the smallest infantry since 1940 and the smallest navy since 1915. He has also removed all tanks from Europe and missile defense especially for Poland. (If you remember the invasion of Poland began World War II).

Plus he has emasculated America's armed forces by promoting the gay lifestyle and authorizing gay marriage.

But don't laugh at America, once the greatest nation on earth, for all that these deceived Muslim prayers of Muslim school children and Muslim immigrants from Palestine, Iraq, Syria, Somalia and other Muslim lands have given us is the disgrace of the Muslim Obama.

Soon and very soon those millions of Muslim immigrants in Western Europe will give to the world through their deceived prayers and votes the horror of the Antichrist, known to them as the twelfth Imam! WAKE UP and EXPECT WAR as it's on the way. The Lord Jesus in the Bible (Mathew 24) says that before He comes again WARS will come. So EXPECT WARS!

Obama's One World Order, Agenda 21, Political Correctness has allowed the enemies of the Gospel of Christ (Jihadist Muslims) to have freedom of religion to impose their evil practices (Shari Law) right here in America to curse our land.

Recently when the Muslims demonstrated for Sheri law in Australia, the Prime Minister of Australia told the Muslims there: 'If you don't like our laws, leave'! Hopefully after this reprobate Obama leaves office, this political correct mess and Jihadist Muslims will also get thrown out with the Obama trash too.

This is where the new prophetic book: <u>The Harbinger</u> by Rabbi Jonathon Chan comes in. This prophetic book (<u>The Harbinger</u>) discloses from scripture **(Isaiah 9:10)** in detail the nine harbingers coming America's way, now that it is under judgment and has been so since the 9/11 tragedy.

This judgment is due to turning away from God just like ancient Israel did. So God's many blessings have now been replaced with judgment.

America's failure to repent of its personal sins like abortion and of social sins like condoning the immigration of Jihadist Muslims has now increased that judgment just as the nine Harbingers indicated so expect more and more damaging tornadoes, more untimely snowstorms and blizzards, more flooding, more unexplained hurricane force winds, more and stronger hurricanes, more severe droughts and more plant diseases as God's judgment expands into plagues that will cause crops to rot in the field and deprive illegal aliens of farm work and Americans of food. This will be Obama's legacy.

These next points are for the benefit of the low information Christian, American citizen and voter who have been too busy trying to earn a living to notice or even care that they have been deceived.

There is one more truth that I must share. This one signifies rebellion against God, the sin of witchcraft, akin to voodoo. In this last election 93% of all Blacks in America voted for Obama, the abortionist. **This means that many so called Christian Church Members cared more for phony chocolate (Obama) than the truth of God's word.** When Christian people deliberately go against the Bible teachings of God heard in Churches across America to follow after phony chocolate instead, then their god has become their belly and every church has a duty to exercise church discipline and excommunicate them or put them out of the fellowship unless they repent.

Now that I have said what God wanted me to say about that, since this book is not a political commentary but a Christian guide on what to expect and since I would rather exonerate someone then to have to constantly expose them and since the more you expose Obama, the more he stinks. Let's just flush this Obama mess and get back to the Evangelist, Jimmy Swaggart.

Some may be disappointed as this evangelist supposedly fell into sin years ago and may feel that such disqualifies him from further Christian ministry now. **'But the gifts and callings of God are without repentance' (Romans 11:29).** So this man still has the Spirit of Truth in him which we can all benefit from. Let him speak truth to us as the oracle of God that he is on all evangelical issues.

When it comes to prophecy however he does not interpret tongues given as prophetic words in his church services, so the dispensing of first hand end time prophetic truth is not his specialty or ministerial calling. As an Assemblies of God minister he just gives out the typical Assemblies of God theological view points on prophetic topics.

Nevertheless, he is one of the three apostolic ministers now broadcasting from America to the whole world today. He can be reached at www.JSM.org or phone 1-800-288-8350. One of the others is Pat Robertson of CBN, and the 700 Club who also heads Regent University in Virginia Beach, Virginia and also operates 'Operation Blessing' for the good of all mankind. His website is WWW.CBN.COM and his phone number is 1-800-759-0700.

The other apostolic leader, Jim Bakker used to head PTL. He served some time in prison for PTL's misdeeds. While there he received visions and wrote his 'prison epistles' about soon coming events and that he had been wrong about both the prosperity message and the pre-tribulation rapture. And he received additional visions after he was released from prison on parole. So thanks to his personal repentance he has now received a new mandate from God by which he has been commissioned

91

to save much people alive by helping them prepare for the hard times of tribulation that's coming our way. He even has a new book out now called: <u>TIME HAS COME</u>. He can be reached at: The Jim Bakker Show. Com or by phoning him at 1-888-988-1588 to buy some of his food-stuff that we'll all soon need as Obama's stupid policies brings God's judgment upon America.

Over the Jim Bakker Show on April 17, 2013 the Christian Prophet John Paul Jackson said; 'The president that God really wanted America to have in 2012 had been aborted in 1972'. Then he said that: 'the man of God tells the truth even if it's inconvenient to tell the truth'.

From what I remember of John Paul Jackson he was typically more direct than the other prophets who had come to visit us at the Vineyard in Anaheim, California back at the end of the 1980's.

John Wimber the pastor of that main Vineyard in Anaheim had invited this prophetic team from Kansas City, Missouri to minister to us. From what I remember their prophetic team was made up of Paul Cain, Rick Joiner, John Paul Jackson and Bob Jones.

Bob Jones looked like a real prophet though (he had silver-grey hair) and he called the exact date of the San Francisco earthquake. Moreover he also said how that it would be seen worldwide. Many thought that was extravagant but a football game was on TV worldwide at the time. So that prophecy rang true.

John Paul Jackson was much younger in those days with long black hair. Some in the congregation said that he was also too good looking to be a real prophet. In any case his clear, direct and outspoken nature was still the same over the Jim Bakker Show. Only this time he looked more like a real prophet with grey hair.

Back in those days I was one of the congregational prophets (those who prophesied to the congregation of the Anaheim Vineyard).

But this visiting team of professional prophets were all nationally recognized. Some of them had been on radio and TV. And a few of them had written books that had been published.

I liked John Paul Jackson the most because of the direct words he shared. He had obviously not been co-opted by having to be politically correct.

I liked the prophet Paul Cain the least because his main concern was about tithing. John Wimber had come out of the Quaker denomination which does not believe in nor practice tithing. Quakers shake; they do not pick anybody's pocket. So most of Paul Cain's message fell flat there in Anaheim.

By the way, before I move on to something else some may wonder how Jimmy Swaggart, an evangelist could possibly operate in an Apostolic ministry. God showed me something about this back in the 1980's after I had become wheelchair disabled and could no longer work and decided to further my education by going to Fuller Theological Seminary after I graduated college in Florida.

I wound up going to Fuller Seminary because the day I went to take my graduate record exam after graduating from college in Florida, early that morning someone had left their stereo on and it was playing an old surfer tune called: 'The little old lady from Pasadena,' and Fuller Seminary is in Pasadena, California. So I went there as I took that song to be my clear word from God to go there.

While there this controversy over Jimmy Swaggart's sexual sin happened and some of my professors started to ridicule me too because they knew that I also was a Pentecostal person. I remember that I fought back though, which most Christians don't do, especially to those who are over you in the Lord. I told them that although I'm not an AG (Assemblies of God) person, nevertheless I'm not gonna let someone talk down one of my brothers for whom Christ has died.

Then I hit them with a word of knowledge I had just gotten back then. I told them that Jimmy Swaggart is a Southern gentleman who needed sexual release, not somebody with a sexual problem anyway. Rather than force sex on the mother of his children, he'd rather have anonymous sex with some mistress like other Southern gentlemen have done. You men of God know full well from the scriptures that some of the heroes of the faith not only had multiple wives but also concubines. (Solomon the wisest man that ever lived had 700 wives and 300 concubines, **I Kings 11:3)**. Since there is nothing new under the sun, **(Ecclesiastes 1:9)** a man's sexual needs back then are still the same today.

Anyway this whole issue comes down to ministerial jealousy. Another minister took pictures of Jimmy Swaggart at a brothel in New Orleans and circulated those pictures in an effort to destroy Jimmy Swaggart's ministry. It's dangerous to attack God's ministers even if your information is correct. So I left this issue there at that time and went on to do my studies.

Several years later God reminded me about this again and also said this to me: 'IN THIS WORLD AND AMONG HIS OWN PEOPLE, JIMMY SWAGGART WILL CONTINUE TO BE KNOWN AS AN EVANGELIST. BUT IN THE KINGDOM OF HEAVEN HE SHALL BE PROMOTED AND GIVEN THE HIGH HONOR OF BEING RECOGNIZED AS THE APOSTLE OF THE CROSS SINCE HIS CONSTANT PREACHING ABOUT THE BLOOD SACRIFICE OF THE LORD JESUS ON THE CROSS GREATLY PLEASES ME.'

Some may want to discount this and say it cannot be a real 'word of knowledge'. To those who feel that way understand this: Jimmy Swaggart is a singer, right. Now singing is a gift, right. When one has this gift but steps back to let others exercise their gifting to sing instead of showing himself off isn't that what the scripture calls **'preferring one another'(Romans 12:10)?** I think that God knows the man's heart full well. And whatever reward He wants to give to anyone, I say, thank you Jesus.

While I was at that school some years ago Pat Robertson was also young and ventured into prophecy by falsely stating that the Soviets would invade Israel and set off Armageddon. He declared this back in May 1982 and also said that by the fall of that year there would be judgment on the world. Although his attempt at prophecy did not materialize back then, nevertheless the man conveys much needed truth that the Spirit of God wants said today for the benefit of all. His 'words of knowledge' encourage many to reach out and receive from God. He can be reached by contacting him at WWW.CBN.COM or 1-800-759-0700.

We've got to get over this mindset of wanting to throw out the baby with the bathwater. We need to accept those Christian Ministers who may be failing people but God has sent them to help us get ready and prepared for the last days now upon us. And reject those reprobates like the Muslim Obama and his Czars that God has not given us but have been fostered up on us both by the seducing spirits of socialism and the evil spirits of deception which made many believe that Obama was 'good chocolate' when his socialist policies have revealed him to be just something a dog has dropped.

This last Obama czar of EBOLA is a political hact and a lawyer master of deceit. As you know lawyers are trained liars. Haven't we already had enough lies from the Obama administration about EBOLA?

Speaking of lies I now remember how that a liberal newspaper from up North published an article naming over 100 lies given by the Obama Administration to the American people just about Obama Care alone. You may even remember one of those lies which said that; 'if you like your doctor, you can keep him'.

Now with EBOLA the official lie is: 'closing the borders will be counter-productive to peoples movement from the EBOLA zone necessary for both world trade to keep these nations solvent and from getting the medical treatment of necessity for EBOLA'. But the truth is most Black African dictators have closed their borders to any and all EBOLA zone travelers. Does the Muslim Obama a half breed Black man have more common sense in this matter than these Black African dictators just because he is an elected democrat?

It is very significant that this last EBOLA czar used to be the political mouthpiece of vice president Biden. Perhaps Obama is paving the way for Biden to take over. But Biden cannot take on Obama's job unless Obama dies in office.

As a nominal Muslim, Obama has absorbed into his subconscious the need for Muslim suicide. Thus he may consider suicide once he realizes that the new Republican Senate will stop this socialist agenda and already has more than enough evidence to impeach him.

In any case all should now see clearly that the Black man 'Duncan' who lied about not being exposed to EBOLA in order to get on the plane and come to America also died here as **'The wages of sin is death'.** But he only told one lie. What judgment now awaits the Muslim Obama and his many czars for telling thousands of lies about 'everything under the sun' to the American people in six years in office?

Muslim Obama's Muslim Deception

1. I told you in my former chapter about Muslim Obama's Deception that Obama is still a nominal Muslim. And there is no record that he was ever converted to Christianity. Complete with a baptism certificate issued by any Christian Church or Christian community of faith.

Muslims are allowed by their false doctrine to conceal, disguise or hide their personal beliefs, Ideas, feelings and opinions in order to achieve personal success for the Muslim cause. Like ruling over Christians or even hiring other Muslims like Valerie Jarrett as public employees to abuse Christians and promote Iran's nuclear arms as well.

Consequently one leading newspaper (it may have been the Washington Post) recently reported over a hundred lies about Obama Care alone. You may even remember one of those lies yourself: 'If you like your doctor, you can keep him'.

Now in the Iran nuclear agreement the Muslim liar Obama is trying to deal with the Muslim liars of Iran. This agreement has to be bad as two lies do not make truth and two wrongs do not make a right!

To make my disclosure about Muslim lying clearer, it must be reiterated that as long as a Muslim is in a country where Islam is a minority, then the Muslim (in this case, Obama's) deceptiveness about anything is officially expected and sanctioned by the 'evil religion of Islam' (the Muslim faith).

2. Obama is really a nominal Muslim by birth and not a Christian at all. Since there is no Record that Obama was ever baptized Christian in any Christian Church. So Obama is an undocumented phony Christian just like all these illegal aliens are undocumented false Americans. (No baptism certificate – no Christian, no birth certificate – no American).

You Afro Americans probably find yourselves more disappointed in your unemployment today than when Obama first took office. Well Obama's priorities have just overshadowed your need for jobs. After all he was so busy doing evil like bailing out the banks, signing anti-American trade agreements, vetoing the Keystone Pipeline and supporting gay marriage that he just had no time to concern himself with 'Black issues'. Like the real social justice of unemployment.

I remember and you probably do too that Dr. Martin Luther King Jr. had a dream where he was looking forward to the time when a man would be judged by the content of his character and not by the color of his skin. **But 93% of all Blacks voted for Obama because they thought that as a Black man, he would see things from a Black perspective.**

Unfortunately for all Americans, Obama is a Black African Muslim descendant from the same Black African Muslims who sold their Black brothers into slavery, since that's what Muslims do just as ISIS showed us. And not an Afro-American Christian at all. Muslim Obama's deception has now turned Dr. Martin Luther King Jr.'s dream into a Muslim socialist nightmare complete with demonic despotism masquerading as 'the beautiful (Muslim) religion'. Therefore now it's time for you to repent and for Muslim Obama to be impeached!

3. On page 40 of his book: <u>The Amateur</u>, when Edward Klein asked Dr. Jeremiah Wright, Obama's former racist pastor, if Obama was ever converted from Islam to Christianity. Dr. Wright said: 'That's hard to tell'. Look, if you're saved, you know it, and so does everybody else that's close to you!

So Muslim Obama was never converted from Islam to Christianity. The Bible also says that **'you judge a tree by its fruit' (Matthew 12:33, Luke 6:44).** In that case **America has had two bad presidents in a row. As you know, George W. Bush (Bush 43) lied America into the Iraq war. But**

he also bailed out the banks as if such was Republican. Look, Republicans believe in business. And according to them all legitimate businesses take necessary risks to succeed or not. If they should fail, that's on them, not on the taxpayers to bail them out. So Bush was wrong about this and Obama was also wrong for continuing this anti-American policy. Remember this when this economy fails again.

So now Hillary Clinton is also getting ready to do wrong to the American people too. Her husband, former President Bill Clinton launched his NAFTA trade agreement which turned America's factories into a wasteland called: 'The Rust Belt'. These policies are NOT Democratic. So no Democrat should vote for the liar Hilary Clinton to become America's next president.

And no Republican should vote for Jeb Bush who would do the Iraq war again. Apparently Jeb Bush believes that the head of his brother, President George Bush 43 is worth far more than the innocent heads of Christian children that ISIS has beheaded now that Iraq is lawless thanks to his brother.

Obama's trade policies are also evil. The Bible even says so. It's wrong to bless strangers and curse your own people with unemployment **(I Timothy 5:8) 'If any man provide not for his own, especially for those of his own house, he has denied the faith and is worse than an infidel'.**

4. Obama's personal hypocrisy reminds me of an incident that happened when I was a child. We called a simple young girl that lived by us Reba Residue. Since one day she went home crying to her mother with her face smeared with dog residue. Her simple mother hollered; 'pew, due, residue!'

Then she asked Reba what had happened. Reba said that she found what she thought was chocolate in a neighbor's front yard. Since she was friends with that neighbor's dog she thought that dog wouldn't mind if she ate what she saw that dog drop. But when she picked up what she thought was chocolate it had melted in the sun and ran down her arm and somehow got smeared on her face and then it changed from being chocolate to something that stunk.

Her upset Mother told her to come in right away and take a bath. Well, the child was hurting. So she couldn't say I'm gonna wash your mouth out with soap.

This reminds me of exactly what Obama's election has produced. Here was a man that many Blacks believed was somehow good, sweet, educated, well spoken and chocolate just like them too. But in reality this man turned out to be just something a dog had dropped as his repugnant socialist policies from his deceptive Muslim nature now stunk to high heaven.

5. For example, when Obama first took office Black unemployment was over 15% but he still had the Congress waste a whole term on his socialist Obama care. So that at the start of his second term Black unemployment was now up over 19%. In all this time he has taken over all healthcare, student loans, the auto industry and mortgages in an attempt to change capitalism into Muslim socialism by promoting his Obama care at your expense and also vetoing the Keystone Pipeline to keep the American people from working and busting Social Security by awarding undeserved disability for bums (especially Black and minority bums).

6. If Obama care was so great then how come Democratic Senators and Congressman grant the reward of exemption to Obama care for those businesses that make political contributions to the Democratic Party?

Speaking again of Obama care, there is one issue that has not yet been mentioned. That is Obama care provides for extended life support services for deformed minority babies (particularly those of illegal aliens and Blacks) who will now grow up to become future socialist voters. That your taxes will support since they will never be able to work just like all those illegal alien children.

Social Work Counselors and Ministers who will become Hospital Chaplains are now being trained to council families to pull the plug on granny in order to save Social Security for these deformed minority babies.

How stupid this racist policy is. Yes Obama care hurts the elderly and gives false hope to the deformed. The deformed can't amount to much in life unless they encounter Christian healing. So it also seems dumb to have kicked prayer out of school when such will be necessary for these deformed students to succeed in life. If these people have a right to a public education, than that education has a duty to expose them to whatever Christian gifts like healing that may be available to them in this life.

7. The Muslim Obama by executive order has removed any display of Christianity (like Crosses and God's Ten Commandments) from American society (especially in the military as they might offend Muslims).

8. Muslim Obama, the Democrat let foreclosures and homelessness happen to sabotage the American economy and even paved the way for GE smart meters to spy on your home if you should still have one.

Obama has also stood by as millions of Americans; both White and Black were unfairly driven out of their homes and into homelessness. For those who somehow may still have homes, Obama has given seventy five million of your tax dollars to help GE build smart electric meters that aid burglars in spying on who's home and what electric appliances you have as they 'case' your house.

9. Not satisfied with that, the Muslim Obama was also behind the expansion of the National Security Agency to spy on you as a supposed intrical part of watching out for terrorism.

Speaking of spying, it is now being done at your expense. Your tax dollars are paying for the Utah Data Center of the National Security Agency (NSA). This agency keeps a record of every phone call and internet transaction that you make. And you are not getting your tax money's worth for there is no evidence that their efforts have ever prevented any terrorist attack. For example, where were they when the Boston marathon bombing happened?

This spying is the main enterprise of the 'military, industrial complex' that former president Eisenhower resented. Back in history several of his advisors (those who also wanted him to appoint that liberal Earl Warren) wanted him to move away from relying upon Christian Prophecy to a more secular and industrial spying on the Soviet Union during the cold war. At that time he used to visit a Christian Prophet in Pasadena, California each month to find out what was happening. This worked out well because **'The eyes of the Lord are in every place beholding the evil and the good' (Proverbs 15:3).**

But even so this prophetic spying was replaced with expensive 'military industrial' spying that your tax dollars now pay for. Think of all the billions wasted on spy satellites that you could have used. **A country cannot use Christian methods if it's no longer Christian. So it's time for revival.** It's far better to restore prayer and Bible reading to school and make America Christian again than to have to pay excessive taxes to fund expensive drug rehab with other welfare programs and social services that distribute 'free' condoms and birth control pills at your expense.

10. I think I said in number 2 above that Obama is a nominal Muslim. Actually the radical Muslims consider him to be backslidden. When Muslims backslide they usually fall back into some indigenous natural religion like sun worship. That's probably why all this stimulus money got wasted on solar enterprises like Solindra.

11. Another means of abusing a Christian nation popular with Muslims is subjugation. An old way to do this was by torture (burying a Christian in the sand up to his head and then letting the ants and scorpions bite and sting

him). A modern way to do this is to use 'Common Core' to dumb down the children of the 'infidels' so that they can't compete with Muslims in the global economy. As the Muslim Obama has already been doing with your tax dollars.

Some years ago when this economy first failed the Muslim Obama took a large part of the stimulus money and gave it to the Department of Education to supposedly ensure the continued full employment of teachers. When it was really used for the enforcement of 'Common Core' upon the states. There are even several books about this skullduggery from both a Christian perspective (1-800-288-8350) and a secular (Crimes of the Educators) perspective.

12. If you remember how that Obama promised change from the Bush policies of Middle East War, Guantanamo terrorist imprisonment, using drones to kill civilians and torturing terrorists.

Here is what has really been happening despite Obama's polished rhetoric: the Middle East war in Afghanistan is continuing and now the one in Syria is due to expand. Guantanamo Bay which holds terrorists beyond the reach of America's constitutional law protections remains opened and still in service. The Obama Administration has used a drone to kill an American citizen. And the Obama Administration's ambassador to Libya and several other Americans were killed by Jihadist Muslims because of resentment over Libya being used as a liberated place to now torture terrorists.

The Muslim Obama now sees it to be more advantageous to violate the constitutional, civil and human rights of American Citizens than to throw out the extreme liberal policy of an idealistic pluralistic society complete with Jihadist Muslims (enemies of the people) living among us as mandated by law. Which law is now supreme, the Constitution and freedom of association, or immigration rights with its liberal notion about pluralistic democracy with having to accept Muslim immigrants that curse our land?

13. In fact what constitutes most Christian prayer is for God to bless people physically, socially and financially. But Muslim prayer (like Obama learned) is for vengeance (Sheri Law), 'social justice' (reclaiming Iraq and Syria for Isis), armaments (like nuclear weapons for Iran) and empowerment to fight and behead the enemies of Islam and to accept martyrdom if need be.

Speaking of Muslim prayer it is also obvious that the Muslim child Obama prayed against US forces in Vietnam just like other Muslim students right there in Indonesia where the Muslim Obama grew up. But these prayers didn't seem to work much then. So most Christians would say that this is because the Muslim god Allah is not real but false.

But prayers to a false god cause people like the Muslim Obama to get worked up with the intention to make their prayers come to pass themselves (self fulfilling prophecy). Psychologists say that's what we have here with the Muslim Obama. **(Since Allah can't, Obama will!)** And now subconsciously Obama has cut back America's armaments to the smallest infantry since 1940 and the smallest navy since 1915. He has also removed all tanks from Europe and missile defense especially for Poland. (If you remember the invasion of Poland began World War II).

Plus he has emasculated America's armed forces by promoting the gay lifestyle and authorizing gay marriage.

His Muslim personality has made him an enemy of the American people, since as a Muslim he really hates gays and is just using his promotion of gays to hurt America.

14. Obama's One World Order, Agenda 21, Political Correctness has allowed the enemies of the Gospel of Christ (Jihadist Muslims) to have freedom of religion to impose their evil practices (Shari Law) right here in America to curse our land.

Recently when the Muslims demonstrated for Sheri law in Australia, the Prime Minister of Australia told the Muslims there: 'If you don't like our laws, leave'! Hopefully after this reprobate Obama leaves office, this political correct mess and Jihadist Muslims will also get thrown out with the Obama trash too.

15. Muslim Obama's evil Obama Care so monopolized the US Senate for over a year thanks to Senator Harry Reid, that the Democratic policy of bringing justice to the unlawful use of the National Guard fighting in foolish foreign wars, like the wasteful misadventure in Iraq never got addressed.

Obviously the National Guard's job is to guard the nation of America and the domestic needs of our people here and not run off to foreign lands to fight foreign enemies. This evil practice can only be changed by enacted law that the Democratic Senate bombarded with all this Obama Care deception was not free to do.

16. The Muslim Obama although he is a Spade, does not like to call a Spade a Spade. So he has called Muslim terrorism workplace violence and plain terrorism. By being a Muslim himself he certainly does not want to give the Muslims a bad name.

Muslims are allowed by their false doctrine to conceal, disguise or hide their personal beliefs, Ideas, feelings and opinions in order to achieve personal success for the Muslim cause. Like ruling over Christians or even hiring other Muslims like Valerie Jarrett as public employees to abuse Christians and promote Iran's nuclear arms as well.

17. The Muslim Obama who represents Islam as 'a religion of peace' has used your tax dollars to arm with outlawed killer bullets most agencies of the Federal Government that have no police power or any right under the law to engage in armed conflict or to police the public and thus need Bush's continued policy of militarizing local police forces.

18. Muslims, like the Muslim Obama like to take over a nation of 'infidels' secretly. So the Muslim Obama has used your tax dollars to secretly supply underground bases to safeguard himself and other Muslims along with the 'useful idiots' of Washington's bureaucrats from whatever social unrest they may cause.

19. The Muslim Obama, resenting 'infidel' military leadership has fired most of America's experienced generals who know how to fight and win. And has replaced them with psychological misfits who lack enough testosterone to even swat a mosquito let alone win a war.

20. But don't laugh at America, once the greatest nation on earth, for all that these deceived Muslim prayers of Muslim school children and Muslim immigrants from Palestine, Iraq, Syria, Somalia and other Muslim lands along with deceived Blacks have given America is the disgrace of the Muslim Obama.

Soon and very soon those millions of Muslim immigrants in Western Europe will give to the world through their deceived prayers the horror of the Antichrist, known to them as the twelfth Imam! WAKE UP and EXPECT WAR as it's on the way. The Lord Jesus in the Bible (Mathew 24) says that before He comes again WARS will come. So EXPECT WARS!

Muslim Jesus vs. Jesus Christ

I had already written the first 2 pages of this chapter. While I was reviewing them. The Lord told me that they were both too soft and too pleasing to the people. He reminded me that He originally said that this book would not be 'politically correct'. Nor is it written 'to win friends and influence people'.

These issues must be confronted by **the sword of the Spirit which is the word of God (Ephesians 6:17).**

Then he told me exactly how to proceed: What the Muslims say is to be presented first. Then the Christian scriptural response is to be given three Fold. One verse is to be given from the King James Version of the Bible. Then one verse from the Amplified Bible and finally one verse from the King James Version of Jimmy Swaggart's Expositors Study Bible. With commentary if it makes the verse clearer.

The first issue to be discussed is that Jesus is the Son of God. Muslims do not believe nor allow anyone to teach that Jesus is the Son of God. To them, their god; Allah doesn't need a son to do his work.

The Muslim Koran pronounces a curse on those who believe that Jesus is God's Son.

In fact, the Muslim Dome of the Rock in Jerusalem has the following words inscribed around the inside of its dome; 'Far be it from God that he should have a son'. With this kind of anti-Christian propaganda this Mosque should have been destroyed in 1967 that the new Jewish Temple may have been built there as Jewish Temples are for God's service not for the exhibiting of anti-Christian hate speech. All temples lift up, praise and glorify some god in some way. Even Temples to false gods do such. No real temple of any god instead of glorifying its own god condemns the real God we may all have to face someday.

Another point to bring this issue to your attention that Muslims apparently have written their main teachings from an attempt to discredit Christian doctrine is their disbelief in the Trinity to the extent that they go out of their way to specifically call such blasphemy in their 'Holy books'.

To Christians the Old Testament King James Bible **asks about God's Son if we know who He is (Proverbs 30:4)**

To Christians the New Testament Amplified Bible says in **I John: 5:12 'He who possesses the Son of God has life and he that does not possess the Son of God does not have that life'.** Isn't that truth plain and clear enough for you?

To Christians the New Testament, King James version of Jimmy Swaggart's Expositors Study Bible says in **Colossians 1:14, that He (God) has translated us into the kingdom of His dear Son.** And not into a Muslim caliphate. Could it be any clearer?

The second issue to be discussed is that Muslims do not believe that the Muslim Jesus died on the cross for our sins. Or that He is in anyway a savior.

But the Bible in the Old Testament King James version calls God: **'The Holy One of Israel our savior' in Isaiah 45:15.** And to Christians of course Jesus is God. The King James Version of the Amplified Bible says in **first John 2:2 'That He (Jesus) is the atoning sacrifice for our sins and not for ours only but also for the sins of the whole world'.** And from Jimmy Swaggart's Expositors Study Bible, King James version, **Colossians 1:20: 'And having made peace (with God) through the blood of His cross by Him (Jesus) all things are reconciled to God.**

Our third issue to consider here is the outlandish Muslim claim that Jesus returns as a radical Muslim.

The very idea that Jesus, the Lord of Glory, the King of Kings should return not to rule and reign **'over every nation, kingdom tribe and tongue'** as recorded in **Revelation 19:16** of any Bible. But to kill every non Muslim like the radical Muslims ISIS is abhorible, revolting and false.

The prophet Isaiah speaking of this time in **Isaiah 2:4** in the Old Testament of any Bible says that '**all shall beat their swords into plow shares and their spears into pruning hooks. Nation shall not lift up sword against nation, neither shall they learn war anymore'**. That does not sound like any radical Muslim killers will be around to kill by beheading all non-Muslims, now does it?

The very idea that the Lord Jesus should return as a radical Muslim like ISIS is not only repulsive but against the prophetic word of God.

In Jimmy Swaggart's Expositors Study Bible, Muslims should realize that the Lord Jesus judges everyman for every sin and **'whomsoever is not found written in the book of life will be cast into the lake of fire, Revelation 20:15'.**

The only way to get recorded in that book of life is to be saved from the consequences of your sins and to receive Jesus not just as savior but also as Lord. And if you obey Him in this life so that **'when He returns (you) shall be rewarded as He shall give to every man according to his works, Revelation 22:12'** the Amplified Bible.

But the Jimmy Swaggart's Expositors Study Bible gives more detail about Jesus coming on page 2100. It says that **'God was manifest in the flesh'** (incarnated) **'justified in the Spirit'** (vindicated, endorsed, proved, and pronounced by the Holy Spirit) **'seen of angels'** (Angels witnessed his birth, life, passion, resurrection and ascension). **'Preached unto the gentiles'** (preached unto the nations that his atonement was for all mankind) **'believed on in the world'** (accepted by many) **'received up into Glory'.** (His mission was accomplished, finished and accepted in total by God). **I Timothy 3:16.**

The fourth issue to be discussed here is the stupid Muslim claim that Jesus is inferior to or subservient to their Mahdi.

The Muslim Mahdi was first mentioned by a former President of Iran as the one who will change the world into a godly paradise. How can a false god do such by beheading Christians and Jews?

The prophet Joel mentions the coming of the Lord in chapter 2 of his Bible book. And he goes on to discuss in chapter 3 of his Bible book the judgments God will bestow on the enemies of his people. Perhaps it would be wise for Muslims to read these verses themselves before they become deceived into believing that their Mahdi or any man or spirit outranks the Lord Jesus Christ, **God manifested in the flesh, I Timothy 3:16.**

The New Testament of the Amplified Bible says: '**that many shall come in Christ's name** (propagating the name that belongs to him) **and shall deceive many**'. Is the Muslim Mahdi one of these impersonators?

But the Jimmy Swaggart's Expositors Study Bible gives more detail about Jesus coming on page 2100. It says that '**God was manifest in the flesh**' (incarnated) '**justified in the Spirit**' (vindicated, endorsed, proved, and pronounced by the Holy Spirit) '**seen of angels**' (Angels witnessed his birth, life, passion, resurrection and ascension). '**Preached unto the gentiles**' (preached unto the nations that his atonement was for all mankind) '**believed on in the world**' (accepted by many) '**received up into Glory**'. (His mission was accomplished, finished and accepted in total by God). **I Timothy 3:16.**

The fifth issue to be discussed here is the stupid Muslim belief that Jesus comes again to enforce Shari Law all over the world.

This would require the Lord Jesus to be a celestial cop with a badge and police power to arrest with mace, a stun gun and a service revolver to then abuse with police brutality any non-Muslims. This obviously is an insult to the divine nature of God.

Law is the concrete of any society. Like for most Muslims, law = Shari Law. For the Romans, law = Roman law. And for English speaking nations, law = English common law. There is not now any one law for all.

But to arrest every non-Muslim for violating Sheri Law like the radical Muslims ISIS is abhorible, revolting and false.

The very idea that the Lord Jesus should return as a radical Muslim like ISIS to enforce Muslim Shari Law is not only repulsive but against the prophetic word of God.

Most Muslims are Arabs used to living in sandy places. But Jesus will not be building his house upon the sand for the wind to abuse but on a solid rock, as it is written in **Matthew 7:26-27: 'and everyone that hearth these sayings of mine, and doeth them NOT shall be like unto a foolish man, which built his house upon the sand. And the rain descended, and the floods came, and the winds blew and beat upon the house: and it fell: and great was the fall of it'.**

In those same verses in the Amplified Bible it says: **'and everyone who hears these words of Mine and does NOT do them will be like a stupid (foolish) man who built his house upon the sand. And the rain fell and the floods came and the winds blew and beat against that house. And it fell and great and complete was its fall'.**

Jimmy Swaggart's Expositors Study Bible comments on these verses by saying in verse 26: (but for the foundation, this house looked the same as the house that was built upon the rock). And in verse 27: (while the sun shines, both houses look good; but when adversity comes and come it shall, *Faith, which is alone in Christ and Him Crucified will stand (I Corinthians 1:18).*

Our sixth issue to discuss is the false Muslim prophecy that Jesus will return to declare himself a Muslim. And He will lead many Christians to convert and become Muslims too. Those who will not convert, he will judge.

Muslims go on to say in their Koran that the people of scripture (Christians and Jews) on the day of resurrection He (Jesus) will be a witness against them (Sura 4:159).

This shows clearly that Muslims twisted the Christian Scriptures that already existed in order to make their perverted (antichrist) claims. What need would the King of Glory have to become a Muslim? If you are the King of a kingdom already it will be empty if you and your Christian people desert it for another.

Now let's confront this false Muslim prophecy. After Jesus was crucified on the cross (for your sins) and rose from the dead and ascended into heaven, angels standing by Him said in **Acts 1:11 'Ye men of Galilee why stand ye gazing up into heaven this same Jesus. . . . .'**

The word 'same' indicates not just similarity but congruence. In other words, exactly now as before (no change in anyway). Consequently the idea that the King of Kings returns as a deceived Muslim to ensure Muslim evangelism to the Christian's own detriment is inconsistent with reality.

The Amplified Bible says that this verse means to them that Jesus will return in like manner as you have seen Him go. Apparently to them the word 'same' means the same method of transport.

But the same method of Jesus transport is already described in the sentence, So, the word 'same' modifies Jesus, not how He gets around. This is why it's necessary to have the Jimmy Swaggart Expositors Study Bible.

The Jimmy Swaggart Expositors Study Bible says that the word 'same' refers to the Person (Jesus) in this case and they go on to say that 'same' refers to Jesus having the same human body with the nail prints in his hands and feet.

This is very important because if Jesus were not a Muslim before his death, He could not be a Muslim evangelist after his crucifixion, resurrection, ascension and second coming in order to be *the 'same' Jesus.*

Our seventh issue to discuss examines that Muslims go beyond their previous false prophecy to say that Jesus also returns to abolish Christianity entirely.

And that he will break all crosses, kill all swine and other things. And will proceed to insult the Christian faith just like a hedonistic spoiled child. In fact that's what the Muslim who wrote this childish insult must be – just a spoiled brat wanting to play Jihad.

The Lord Jesus will not be coming back to abolish Christianity but to confirm it by rewarding it. In fact **He says that His reward is with Him Revelation 22:12.**

A reward is something to cherish not something that gets abolished and thrown out in the trash. The Amplified Bible of Revelation 22:12 says: **'I shall bring my wages and rewards with me; to repay and render to each one just what his own actions and his own work merit'.**

And Jimmy Swaggart's Expositors Study Bible says: **'My reward is with me** (the word reward can either be positive or negative) **to give every man according as his work shall be** (our faith however placed will produce a certain type of works. *Only faith in the cross is accepted*).

Our eighth issue to discuss is the false Muslim claim that the Muslim Jesus is a primary instigator of the final war. This does not sound like a proper vocation for the Prince of Peace, now does it? The scripture says in **Romans 5:1: 'therefore being justified by faith, we have peace with God through our Lord Jesus Christ'.**

That same verse, **Romans 5:1**: says in the Amplified Bible: **'Therefore being justified by faith, we have peace with God, through our Lord Jesus Christ'** (The Messiah, the anointed one).

And in Jimmy Swaggart's Expositors Study Bible **(Romans 5:1) Therefore being justified by faith let us have the**

peace of reconciliation with God through our Lord Jesus Christ (this is the only way one can be justified refers to *faith in Christ and what he did at the cross***).**

So far this chapter has only dealt with Muslim false doctrine. We will return to that in a moment. But first God wants me to deal with the evil Muslim cultural deception that discriminates against women.

The authorized King James Bible says in **I Corinthians 11:10** that: **'A woman ought to have power over her own head** (Not some Muslim family nor some Muslim authority) **because of the angels'** (who are higher in authority than any imam).

Then it goes on to say in **I Corinthians 11:15** that **'If a woman have long hair it is a glory to her'** (her natural God given covering). In order for her to be attractive her beautiful long hair must be exhibited openly and not hidden beneath an artificial man made covering like a Muslim Hijab, Niqab or Burka.

A normal man likes to show off his wife. In some cultures the wife wears the family heirlooms, gold and diamond necklaces. And in primitive cultures rare sea shells of what her husband caught or even the trophies of animals that her husband killed in battle for food.

No normal man hides his wife. To do so indicates a psychological problem.

Our tenth issue to discuss is the Muslim claim that the Muslim Jesus will return to earth at some Mosque in Damascus. He will arrive just in time to meet the Muslim Mahdi to prepare for the final war.

The Scriptures however state that **'Jesus feet will stand that day on the Mount of Olives which is before Jerusalem on the East', Zachariah 14:4.**

Jimmy Swaggart's Expositors Study Bible says that this will be His landing point at the second coming.

Speaking of Damascus, the prophet Isaiah says in **Isaiah 17:1** that 'Damascus shall be taken away from being a city, and it shall become a ruinous heap'.

Then the Amplified Bible wants us to cry a dirge over it for **'Damascus would cease to be a city and will become a heap of ruins' the Amplified Bible, Isaiah 17:1**. Damascus will be the capitol of Syria when this happens. And that did not happen until 1946. So it must be destroyed sometime soon. Then this false Muslim prophecy shall also find the ruin it deserves for twisting the word of God.

Our eleventh issue to be discussed is the false Muslim belief that the Zionist Empire of Israel will fall and the religion of Islam will prevail since the Muslim Jesus never really liked the Jews anyway.

Jesus (the prince of peace) now supposedly Muslim will fight against Zionist Jews (His own people) according to the Muslims.

How stupid this Muslim false teaching is for anyone can see for themselves from any Bible that the New Testament begins in **Matthew 1:1** with the genealogy of Jesus Christ clearly showing Christ's Jewish ancestry.

Contrary to what Muslims believe, Israel is due to expand to the original borders that God gave Abraham in **Genesis 15:18.**

Jimmy Swaggart's Expositors Study Bible says in **Genesis 15:19 that 'Abraham will be given all that land from the river of Egypt (Nile) unto the great river, the river Euphrates'** (the actual area promised by God to Abraham goes all the way to the Nile river in Egypt which includes Sinai, the Arab Peninsula, then up to much of modern day Iraq, most of Syria and all of Lebanon and Jordan too).

Our twelfth issue to discuss is that the Muslim Jesus = the Biblical false prophet.

Muslims use Jesus as a lure to draw Christians in.

The Biblical false prophet can also perform miracles. So Muslims do not believe that their healing or any miracle evidences the Jesus of the Bible but the counterfeit Jesus of Muslim false doctrine. Consequently if I were a faith healer or Christian miracle worker I would not go to Muslim lands to minister to Muslims or to associate with and befriend them. In **Ephesians 5:11** the Bible says: '**Have no fellowship with the unfruitful works of darkness but rather reprove them'.** Muslims just corrupt your Christ; don't give them the ammunition to do so.

One famous Christian healer, Norvel Hayes performs mighty miracles and healings by the laying on of hands (a Christian Biblical doctrine). The Muslim false prophet also performs miracles. So does their Dajjal or Antichrist. In fact he heals the sick by wiping his hands in them just like Jesus did. Do you want to have any part in such a fraudulent 'beautiful religion'?

Since some of you have already fallen for this politically incorrect plural democracy propaganda about accepting Muslims into your communities and nations, I need to share this Bible verse with you: **II Corinthians 5:14 ' Be not unequally yoked together with unbelievers; For what fellowship has righteousness with unrighteousness; and what communion has light with darkness'.**

The Amplified Bible elaborates further by saying**: 'Do not be unequally yoked with unbelievers'** (do not make mismated alliances with them or come under a different yoke with them inconsistent with your faith)! **'For what fellowship has righteousness with unrighteousness';** (and right standing with God with inequity and lawlessness)? **'Or how can light have fellowship with darkness'.**

Do you now understand what the Bible and me are saying? If so, let's now move on to discuss our next issue.

Our thirteenth issue to discuss is will the Antichrist Empire be Muslim?

Muslim deceit and trickery more than any religion, philosophy, ideology or belief system exhibits the antichrist spirit complete with brimstone breathe. I mentioned somewhat about this in the chapter about the Byzantine Empire. As you probably remember Byzantine was the eastern part of the Roman Empire which fell to the Muslim Ottoman Turks in 1453.

For our purposes the Empires of man are those which control Jerusalem (the center of God's Earth). So first came Egypt then Assyria then Babylon then Medo-Persia then Greece then Rome then the Muslim Ottoman Turks.

There is scripture that says that the last Empire shall be revived to become the Antichrist Empire. Before this book, most theologians and church historians believed that the last empire to be revived would be Rome. But history shows that it will be the Muslim Turks instead.

All of the current western democracies that were once part of Rome, now have significant Muslim Turkish population. A historian from England now says that there are more Mosques in England than churches and that England will no doubt become Muslim shortly after his death.

If democracy is to prevail then the rule of the majority will give these Muslim Turks rule over you. So then expect Muslim rule along with the beheadings of Christians. It's coming for sure. The Bible says so **(Revelations 20:4) 'I saw the souls of them that were beheaded for the witness of Jesus'.**

Our fourteenth issue to discuss is was Mohamed demonic?

Actually Mohamed is in good company here since Jesus too was also accused of being demonically inspired for healing on the Sabbath day (**Luke 13:10-17**). Jesus was also accused by the Pharisees of casting out devils through the prince of the devils **(Matthew 9:34, Matthew 12:24, and Mark 3:22).**

Mohamed however never healed anyone. Neither did he cast out devils. Perhaps he couldn't cast devils out because he had one. What other reason is there for his attacks on Christianity?

But Jesus never killed anyone or exhorted his followers to kill. Plus Jesus never lied about anything to anyone. In fact Jesus kept the law of God blamelessly.

Mohamed claims that he was on his way to commit suicide when he heard a voice from heaven saying: 'O Mohamed! Thou art the Apostle of God and I am Gabriel'. Gabriel announces good news, like he foretold the birth of Jesus Christ **(Luke 1:30-37).** To negate that by calling Mohamed an Apostle makes Gabriel a two faced, double talker (an insane murderer is not an apostle).

There is no Bible record of Gabriel ever telling anyone what their ministerial spiritual gift will be. So the idea of Gabriel calling Mohamed an Apostle is false. Even the Mormons (an American false religious cult) had enough sense to call their angel giving them a different gospel a different name: (Moroni).

By using Biblical figures to confirm their false doctrine just shows that Islam is an antichrist religion. Plus the idea that God would give theological information to someone instead of stopping them from committing suicide is against the nature of God (the life giver).

God usually speaks to people in a gentle way if by angels. In fact, most angels began their speaking by saying: **'fear not'.** To have dark spiritual experiences like Mohamed had in the cave Hira is like the experience of a spiritualist or someone who channels spirits. Since I come from the county in Florida where Cassadaga (the main retirement community of spiritualists) is located, I know something about them. One obvious fact is that any experience from dark spiritual experiences lead to anti biblical revelations and also eventually to killing (like the killing of every Jew, Christian and non Muslim). **It is the devil and not**

Gabriel who leads people to kill, rob and destroy (John 10:10).

As I said before the taking of biblical characters to espouse and to confirm anti biblical false doctrine makes Islam, (the religion of Muslims) antichrist. This should now be plain for all to see, so let's move on to discuss our next issue.

Our fifteenth issue to discuss is another coming Muslim Middle East war.

Contrary to what former president George W. Bush (Bush 43) said Islam is certainly not a religion of peace. Their Holy books say that the Muslim Mahdi will return during troublesome times (no food, water, jobs, money or peace) to wage war against the Jews in Jerusalem, to reconquer it for Islam and to establish a Muslim Caliphate there to rule over the whole earth from Jerusalem. This will happen as his armies carrying black flags will come from Iran to the Dome of the Rock in Jerusalem where they will then erect their black flags as a sign of conquest.

But contrary to this false prophecy, the Bible says in **Genesis 15:18** that Israel is due to expand its borders to the original borders that God showed to Abraham.

Jimmy Swaggart's Expositors Study Bible says in **Genesis 15:19 that 'Abraham will be given all that land from the river of Egypt (Nile) unto the great river, the river Euphrates'** (the actual area promised by God to Abraham goes all the way to the Nile river in Egypt which includes Sinai, the Arab Peninsula, and from there on up to much of modern day Iraq, most of Syria and all of Lebanon and Jordan too).

We'll soon see which prophecy is true and which God is real. I hope that at that time Israel takes it upon itself to use its neutron bomb to eliminate once and for all the Palestinian problem by dropping it on Gaza, Damascus and wherever else it might be appropriate. The Bible says that **'there is a time of war and a time of peace' (Ecclesiastes 3:8).** *It's time to kill the killers!*

Our sixteenth issue concerns the Muslim weapon of mass destruction called: killing (beheadings, homicide and suicide).

Previously we discussed Mohamed's attempt at suicide. I could have used a whole page to condemn Mohamed but that's not my purpose right now. As I feel that if something is truly of God no one can fight against it and if not it will come to naught. When we discussed Mohamed some in our fourteenth issue and mentioned his attempt at suicide, some unexpected truth came before me.

As you know many former US soldiers are now returning from Iraq to commit suicide once home in America.

Former President George W. Bush (Bush 43) as I said before failed to have necessary biblical scholars with knowledge of Biblical prophecy to advise him about the Iraq war. Consequently (Bush 43) sent our young men to get even for 9 11 and to supposedly extend democracy to that demon infested land.

Even Mohamed was attacked by demons of suicide himself in Arabia, the dry and thirsty land that demons love.

But Iraq is far worse when it comes to demon possession since there are demons in Iraq under the Euphrates River who have been given the right to kill 1/3 of mankind **(Revelation 9:14 &15)**. Knowing this fact no American soldiers should have been sent to that land for revenge, extension of democracy or any other reason, certainly not for a Muslim girl's right to get an education our next issue to discuss.

Our seventeenth issue is: is a Muslim girl's education worth your life?

Anyone with any sense would say that women already talk too much about things they don't even know things about. They certainly don't need to know more so that they can talk more.

Today in America and many other nations too, there are more women in college than men, learning more to talk more on cell phones.

Women were given by God as a gift to man **to be man's help meet (Genesis 2:18).** Not to be his dictator or boss.

Just knowing these few facts I would not waste my life for any girls education (certainly not a Muslim girl) Thanks to all these unnecessary and stupid wars there are already far more women than men in every city and town in America. I definitely have no intentions of adding to that statistic.

<u>Our eighteenth issue discloses why Obama is such a bad President: Because he is a Muslim and Muslims even Obama can and do lie!</u>

I told you in my former chapter about Obama's Deception that Obama is still a nominal Muslim. And there is no record that he was ever converted to Christianity complete with a baptism certificate issued by any Christian Church or Christian community of faith.

Muslims are allowed by their false doctrine to conceal, disguise and hide their personal beliefs, Ideas, feelings, and opinions in order to achieve personal success for the Muslim cause. Like ruling over Christians or even hiring other Muslims like Valerie Jarrett as public employees to abuse Christians and promote Muslim Iran as well.

Consequently one leading newspaper (it may have been the Washington Post) recently reported over a hundred lies about Obama Care. You may even remember one of those lies yourself: 'If you like your doctor, you can keep him'.

Now in the Iran nuclear agreement the Muslim liar Obama is trying to deal with the Muslim liars of Iran. This agreement has to be bad as two lies do not make truth and two wrongs do not make a right!

To make my disclosure about Muslim lying clearer, it must be reiterated that as long as a Muslim is in a country where Islam is a minority, then Muslim deceptiveness

about anything is officially expected and sanctioned by the Muslim faith.

You Afro Americans probably find yourselves more disappointed in your unemployment today than when Obama first took office. Well Obama's priorities have just overshadowed your need for jobs. After all he was so busy bailing out the banks, signing anti-American trade agreements, vetoing the Keystone Pipeline and supporting gay marriage that he just had no time to concern himself with 'Black issues' like Black unemployment.

I remember and you probably do too that Dr. Martin Luther King Jr. had a dream where he was looking forward to the time when a man would be judged by the content of his character and not by the color of his skin. But 93% of all Blacks voted for Obama because they thought that as a Black man, he would see things from a Black perspective.

Unfortunately Obama is a Black African Muslim descendant from the same Black African Muslims who sold their Black brothers into slavery, since that's what Muslims do, just as ISIS showed us. And not an Afro-American Christian at all. Muslim Obama's deception has now turned Dr. Martin Luther King Jr.'s dream into a socialist nightmare. Therefore now it's time for you to repent and for the Muslim Obama to be impeached!

Our nineteenth issue concerns the Muslim goal of World domination.

All nations need to take note: Islam, the faith of Muslims, intends to destroy every government made by man, even yours. The goal of this Muslim faith is to rule over the entire world and subject all mankind to its false doctrine.

To all democracies Muslims say that thanks to your democratic laws Muslims shall invade you, and thanks to Muslim religious (Shari) law Muslims shall rule over you!

Islam, the so called religion of peace is now responsible for the most fighting currently occurring in the world. This 'evil religion' motivates the vast majority of terrorists worldwide. Franklin Graham, the son of the famous evangelist Billy Graham called the Muslim faith 'an evil religion'. For that statement of truth he was excluded from Obama's prayer breakfast (since the Muslim Obama only prays to Allah, a false god anyway, 'it's no big deal'.

Many European nations had Muslim demonstrations some years ago in which the Muslims that lived there held signs which said: 'Islam our religion today, your religion tomorrow'. This evil Muslim manifesto of conquest must be crushed by whatever means it takes.

Young Muslims are subsequently told in their 'holy books' to expect warfare because it is ordained for them. And that Allah commands every Muslim to fight unbelievers. According to them killing (Jihad) is an act of worship, 'One of the supreme forms of devotion to Allah, their false god.

This evil Muslim manifesto of conquest must be crushed by whatever means it takes.

According to them fighting (Jihad) is an act of worship.

One way they take over nations today is clearly evident by what they did to Lebanon. There the President must be a Muslim by Constitutional law, while the vice president must be a Christian. Actually then Muslim terrorists took over the country to use its army to fight Israel. And the Lebanese people do without government services. Now this same plan of conquest is getting ready to happen again in Nigeria which suffers from the same Constitutional legal abuse: Muslim President, Christian vice-president.

Our twentieth issue asks which will it be: A Muslim revival or a Christian revival.

1. Islam, the religion of Muslims, is the fastest growing religion in the world.

2. 9 11, the spirit of death, has triggered Muslim growth four fold.

3. Most American Muslims reside in our cities, most in New York City. In fact, by 2020 most American cities will be Muslim.

4. Thanks to Obama, 85% of all American Muslims will be Black.

5. There is a higher birth rate among Black American Muslims than White Americans. (After all, Muslims enjoy four wives).

6. Islam, the religion of Muslims, hopes to be the main instrument of Satan to fulfill Bible prophecies in these last days.

7. Christianity in Latin America, Africa and Asia is now experiencing revival.

8. Many Muslims are now having Christian dreams about Jesus that overshadows their false Muslim doctrine about Jesus not being the Son of God.

9. Through 'the falling away' God is allowing lukewarm or nominal Christians to fall away from the Christian faith, to adopt Islam, the religion of Muslims on their way down to hell.

10. There is much false teaching today from the pacifists that now rule the Christian church that we should just accept this Muslim conquest as the will of God for Christian martyrs.

11. Although the Lord Jesus died for your sins, your blood and life can't save anyone. So why sacrifice yourself? The Lord Jesus did give us an example to follow in his steps, but neither in His passion nor crucifixion.

12. There is much misunderstanding among modern Christians about loving your enemies. The Bible does say to '**love your enemies' (Matthew 5:44).**

13. *But the Bible does NOT say anywhere to love the enemies of God!* '**When the Lord Jesus returns, He will fight against His enemies' (Zachariah 14:1).**

14. The Lord Jesus also said that '**the works that I do shall you do also and greater than these shall you do' (John 14:12).**

15. The Bible goes on to say: '**As He is** (the King of Glory with all enemies under His feet), **so are we in this world' (1 John 4:17).**

16. So God will make your enemies (these radical Muslims) your footstool.

17. As far as Christian revival is concerned remember: '**I can do all things** (win wars against Muslim Jihadists, expose corruption, perform miracles, impart healings, feed multitudes, command storms to be still, make it rain, supply people with jobs and get people saved, sanctified, filled and ready to now serve God) **through Christ Who strengthens me' (Philippians 4:13).**

18. Then the Lord Jesus in the Bible says: '**Render unto Caesar the things that are Caesars and unto God the things that are Gods' (Luke 20:25, Mark 12:17, Matthew 22:21).** Don't get entangled in political controversies that no one can solve, but do the will of God by just obeying Him.

19. '**I'm complete in Him, which is the head of all principality and power' (Colossians 2:10).** So there is no power that I need to be scared of!

20. '**Except the trumpet give a certain sound who shall prepare themselves for battle' (I Corinthians 14:8). <u>Your trumpet call has already been given to you via my prophetic book. What will you now do about it?</u>**

Matthew Chapter 24, Verse 6: 'Wars and Rumors of Wars'.

The next unpleasant event for us to consider is wars in Matthew 24:6.

Some of you have had your great grandparents tell you that during the Second World War food and other things were rationed. Some of those food items rationed at various times included sugar, coffee, tea, butter, milk, rice, beans, cheese and all kinds of meat. Some of those other items rationed included gasoline, clothing, wool and even light bulbs. My mother had to wear cardboard shoes to school because the leather needed for shoes was rationed and there was none to be found. It took the sacrifice of the nation's people to win that war.

It's going to take your sacrifice to also win this one against the devil too. Face it, the Lord Jesus had to experience a blood sacrifice in His own blood. If **the servant is not greater than his Lord (John 15:20)** then similar sacrifice is also coming your way too.

The dictionary says that war is open conflict resulting from hostility. The participants in any war are usually nation states whereas any disagreement resulting in battle between two individuals is just a fight, even if it results from bullying and involves the school board, the authorities like the police, and others like your family or your neighborhood too.

However when a conflict escalates to the point of bombing innocent people as in the Marathon bombing in Boston then that attack constitutes 'an act of war' upon our society. Especially if the bomber admits that the reason why this was done was because of America's war in Iraq that's killing Muslims. In such case the Boston bombing is just an extension of the war in Iraq and the bomber or perpetrator is an enemy combatant not just a criminal bomber.

When I heard the word 'Marathon' of the Boston Marathon bombing it sparked my memory of that word in the history book: <u>Lessons From Fallen Civilizations, Can a Bankrupt America Survive the Current Islamic Threat?</u> By Larry Kelly.

This book points out that the Greeks defeated the Persians at Marathon which was the first resolution by war of their threats against western civilization. The Greeks won because they were more highly skilled, Olympic and athletic runner-warriors armed with long iron tipped pikes. Who as free men both decided and determined to fight to the death if need be to resist the Persians even against overwhelming odds (there were only about 11,000 Greeks against 26,000 Persians).

This book goes on to list 10 reasons why civilizations fall. But I am a prophet not a secretary so it is not my purpose to copy another man's work. As a Christian, I do not steal the ideas of others either. Moreover as a prophet, I like to be original. If you want to know what this man has to say, please buy his book and read it for yourself. His book is profound and it's well worth your money.

My twelve points about why civilizations fall are: **(1) Surviving nations must believe that their culture is worth saving. (2) Warriors must be free men whose fighting is voluntary. (3) Free people do not stay free through taxation. (4) To own a territory, a state must be populated by loyal subjects. 'When immigration overwhelms assimilation' loyalty fades away and the state falls too. (5) With no balanced budget also comes the loss of sovereignty (no money – no statehood). (6) Printing more money (debasing the currency) leads the state to capitulation. (7) To ensure peace, stay strong by having the latest weapons available and if need be use them. Don't let some pacifist emasculate your country. (8) Do not allow your enemies to use freedom of speech to broadcast their propaganda to your people. (9) Stop all Jihadist Muslim immigration to America. (10) Do not allow Jihadist Muslims to have freedom of religion to worship their false god here and thereby curse our land. (11) Put all Jihadist Muslims already here out of the country and if necessary by force. (12) If any war develops anywhere that threatens**

our country or its allies with Jihadist Muslim aggression immediately put those Jihadist Muslims responsible to death by whatever means is necessary.

This verse about wars is most notable for what it does not say. There is no admonition from the Lord about involving yourself in these wars. Neither is there any modification of the word; wars. **Your body is the temple of the Holy Ghost (I Corinthians 6:19).** And not the instrument of some 'democratic' despot who calls himself your president.

A survivalist once told me that I needed to relocate to some place safe from war. He even gave us a website that I still remember; it was WWW.BestPlaces.NET/CITY This website compared many different cities and towns across America. I noticed to my horror that almost all of these locations had a much lower male than female population. So all these wars then are obviously killing our young men! Such destruction of our young men in war is mainly due to the pacifist propaganda behind our failure to use nuclear weapons to blow these reprobates away instead of wasting our young men in hand to hand combat.

Speaking of pacifist propaganda, pacifists now rule the church. With all their lovey-dovey nicey-nicey, turn the other cheek capitulating mind set of surrender. So many Christians are now pacifists and some are even 'gay' Christians too.

But in the Old Testament, **(I Kings 1:10),** a man of God named Elijah had to pronounce judgment on the King of Samaria. Obviously the king was displeased and sent a captain of 50 to apprehend Elijah and bring him back to the king. But Elijah did not care for being seized and said 'If I be a man of God then let fire come down from heaven and consume you and your fifty and it was so'. The king did this again with the same result. But the third time Elijah went to the king of his own free will. And once he got there Elijah pronounced judgment again! The king died right then and there so he was not able to give any orders of retribution.

This is the exact account of judgment we Christians need to see more of today to encourage young Christians to stand up against evil. The king of Samaria was into evil and the worshipping of false gods. Where evil abounds, we don't need to tolerate the worshipping of false gods or child molesting, sexual assaults and reprobates of every stripe.

Most Christian theologians say that the two witness who called down fire from God to burn up this evil were the two Old Testament prophets Moses and Elijah.

So most Christian churches do not believe that any New Testament Christians today can be prophets of power. But we should still believe that if one becomes spiritual enough they could still call down fire from heaven to burn up evil too.

But today spirituality is measured materially as the possession of property especially according to the 'prosperity message'.

The Old Testament also had other heroes of the faith like Samson the Nazirite warrior who had superhuman strength to fight back against the Philistines (the Palestinians of that day). Where are our modern Christian men of war?

Speaking of prophets who will be fighting against evil in our future as I said before most Christian theologians say that these two will be Moses and Elijah.

Excuse me reincarnation is another religion, NOT Christianity! God said to Joshua in Joshua 1:2 that: 'Moses my servant is dead now therefore arise.......'So Moses did not intervene at anytime in Joshua's conquest of the promised land. That burden fell on Joshua alone. Should we now have the gall to expect Moses to fight our battles too?

In considering Elijah his mantle fell to Elisha who did twice as many miracles as Elijah did.

Christian theologians know something about Christian history but since they are not prophets they know little about prophecy.

As a prophet myself, I know that once the mantle on a prophet is transferred to another, their life of prophecy ends.

So Moses and Elijah will **NOT** be coming back to continue fighting for us. Those confrontations recorded in Revelation will be done by young Christians that you have encouraged to get spiritual enough to be used of God to do those things instead of just resigning themselves to beheadings.

One more revelation for you is this one. Given: The Lord Jesus said; **'The works that I do shall you do also and greater than these shall you do' (John 14:12).** Among those many works that Jesus did was feeding the five thousand men from the lunch of a boy amounting to two fish and five loaves.

After the Lord Jesus blessed the loaves and fish He gave them to His disciples who distributed them to the people. After the people were filled, His disciples gathered up discarded fish bones and other fragments enough to fill twelve baskets full.

No church today teaches it's Christians especially those who are going to be missionaries to expect to do such Miracles of Provision like this. In fact in this modern world we call God; Jehovah Jireh, the Lord our Provider but we do not expect supernatural provision.

Instead we go to the store to buy what we need. How will we buy food when no one can buy or sell without the mark of the beast or the number of his name (666)?

We can buy some food beforehand that is preserved to last 20 years by calling 1-888-988-1588. We can also buy some farmland to grow our own food.

In America we are told that only Congress can declare war. If so then how come presidential directives can authorize your participating in 'police actions'? 'Police actions' is just another euphemism for war. So not all wars are legitimate, worthwhile or necessary. Christians have no business sacrificing their lives to ensure the supposed freedom of Muslim woman to be educated.

Nor for anti-Christian Muslims under Sheri law to have the right to vote.

Those who fight for the nation should be in its own armed forces. The job of the National Guard should be guarding their nation, not going off to some foreign nation to fight a bunch of infidel Muslim jihadist there and then rebuild that nation. So then there are obviously hypocritical wars too.

This verse also does not say when you hear of wars, volunteer!

Current wars are in 'the time warp' of current events. Soldiers fight for the nation as it exists now and not to sanction some future social error or deterioration.

(None of the soldiers who fought against the Nazi's in the Second World War fought for their current socialist governments in Europe with the immigration of Black Jihadists Muslims from North Africa). No soldier then fought for the so called future social improvement of nuclear power plants to produce electricity to run all of Europe.

Nor did the Americans who fought and died in that war do so for the integration of schools, legalized mixed marriages, legalized abortions, legalized pot and other dope or even gay marriages. So be very careful that what you sacrifice your life for today may not be worthy of your sacrifice tomorrow as your body is the temple of the Holy Ghost **(I Corinthians 6:19).**

But not all wars can be voted against, protested, or stopped. Some wars are prophetic wars and must happen whether you like it or not. These prophetic wars include those mentioned by the prophets in **Jeremiah 49:34-39, Ezekiel 38 & 39, Isaiah 17 and Psalm 83.**

Now that I am older and have hopefully grown some in the faith. I'm going to follow the example of my brother Apostle Jimmy Swaggart by stepping back to let others with my same prophetic gifting to share whatever God has imparted to them about these prophetic wars. One of these men of God is our brother: Bill Salus whose book: <u>Revelation Road</u> says what our God wants us to know about these wars. He can be contacted at: WWW.PROPHECYDEPOT.COM

Some current prophets and prophetic people say that the psalm 83 war is near at hand. Brother Salus has a book about it (<u>Psalm 83 The Missing Prophecy Revealed</u>). May I also make one suggestion that will probably be called by the liberals my incitement to genocide. Whenever this war breaks out the state of Israel needs to drop a neutron bomb on Gaza to get rid of Hamas and Hezbollah and the Palestinian problem right away before it becomes a state recognized by the UN.

I do not believe and I know that God, the God of Israel does not want any two state solution for Palestine. In fact Israel is due to become much larger in territory than it is now, right after this psalm 83 war most of that land will be the result of conquest.

When Joshua attacked Jericho, he was told by God to slay all men, woman and children and animals. Anti-war liberals call this genocide. But it's really just total war. And if it's not done again Israel will have the Palestinian problem until Jesus comes.

When I was a teenager I had to take the school bus to get to school. That bus usually picked me and others up about a quarter after seven in order to get us to school on time. If that bus was just a few minutes late I remember how we would have to wait at the railroad tracks for the long train to go by before we got to go. Then obviously we'd be late for class.

That long train that went by every morning before 7:30 was the army train. It had about five engines and almost 300 cars loaded with every form of military hardware, from jeeps and missiles to tanks with trucks armed with machine guns and recoilless rifles. The nation was getting ready for war; it was clear and obvious and scared some of us. Although the country prepared for the 'Bay of Pigs' invasion of Cuba, such never materialized as president Kennedy was talked out of providing necessary air cover by the Democratic pacifists of that era. Thus this became just another 'rumor of war'.

Perhaps North Korea's verbal assault today will just be like another 'rumor of war' we once heard about Cuba. Although it appears very threatening, I doubt that anyone wants to go through all the effort and expenditure required to take them out.

Since we had studied American History already in school, I knew that Cuba was won by Americans like Theodore Roosevelt in the Spanish American War of 1898. America gave Cuba its independence in 1926. But now that it had gone astray to adopt stupid communist ideology it was time to take it back, and if necessary by force.

We saw those army trains with weapons. We knew that America had the firepower but it failed to go forth to battle in war when it was well able to win. I hope that the people of God don't make that same mistake. When the trumpet sounds, let's go forth to battle!

The Bible says that there is a time for war and a time for peace. There are two new books about this called: <u>A Time for War</u> and <u>Stop the Coming Civil War</u> both by Dr. Michael Savage. They must be well written and well researched as Dr. Savage is a first rate author whose extensive vocabulary keeps my memory of words active.

Someone once said that war is hell. It has also been said that if just a World War II type conventional war were to break out in Europe today and not a single nuclear weapon was used in battle just the destruction of Europe's nuclear power plants by conventional bombs alone would render all of Europe uninhabitable for tens of thousands of years.

There are over 100 nuclear power plants across America today now too giving out electric power to run all our stuff, but when war comes these same modern wonderworking devices will give us the emaciating death of horror films.

The horrible consequences of having to endure a land war in America has not yet been adequately examined, evaluated and explained. If that war comes, and eventually it will. Then reality will have to be faced.

Since the air may be contaminated with nuclear radiation you may have to breathe through a gas mask if you can find one. If there is no pure water, what will you drink? Since no one has gardens now, where will you find fresh vegetables to eat?

How will you be able to travel with no gasoline, nor electricity to pump the gas? If electricity fails, and it will. How will you get money out of any ATM or bank? What store could open for business if they can't run the electric check out register? How can you learn of emergency news reports with no working TV?

I live in Florida where occasionally hurricanes happen. When the wind starts blowing big time power lines go down and electric current to your house fails. Such means no air conditioning, no electric cooking stove, no TV, no fans, no electric lights to see your way around, no refrigeration to keep your food safe and fresh and no hot water for showers or to do laundry.

Since no stores could open without electricity to run their cashiers, there would be no operating pharmacies to get your medicine, no grocery stores to buy food, no banks to get your money, no service stations to get gas for your car or truck and no gun stores to buy ammunition for your gun to shoot game to survive. In addition to this tragedy no fish stores would be opened to buy bait for fish. In other words you'd be in bad shape if you had not prepared.

Therefore I recommend that you have at least a ninety day supply of prescription drugs for your medical needs. Then get at least a year's worth of food and pure water for yourself and your family by calling 1-888-988-1588 for whatever else maybe available to meet your survival needs.

I had planned to elaborate especially on the main scriptural versus used in my book. However at a little after 5:00pm on

April 26, 2013 I got a phone call from a dental office. I asked them where they were and they said that they were in downtown Chicago on Chicago intersecting la Sale.

I told them that I have no known tooth problems at this time and besides I live in Florida over a thousand miles away. So I wouldn't go up to Chicago for expensive dental care anyway.

Then I hung up. At first I thought that this dumb phone call was just a mistake or a wrong number. But these people knew my name. Plus my phone only makes local calls. I have no long distance service set up. So then I looked at this unexpected phone call as a disguised word from God.

I remembered that I once heard a dental joke which said: with Jesus being substituted for all these chocolate bunnies instead of being recognized as the solution for sins like abortion and gay marriage, maybe we should expect Jesus to return as a dentist with a drill.

Words like this from a dental office usually have some kind of dental meaning. I think I've hit on it right off. Since it had no further confirmation, like a dream from God, therefore it now stands as my first warning and means that I have been given only two years to complete my book and get ready to relocate to the place of safety that God wants me to go to.

From here on out then my research will need to be scaled down, what I can include, I will. The next section on the American Civil War is ready to show you how Americans deal with war in their community. **You'll need to know this for war is coming; the lord Jesus said so in Matthew 24:6.**

The Lord Jesus Christ could have said don't worry about this war stuff because you'll soon be in heaven with Me. But He never made any such statement. Therefore the pre-tribulation rapture viewpoint is American propaganda without any Biblical support.

Some Christians feel that they will never have to endure war since as Christians they are not appointed unto wrath. But the wrath being talked about here is God's wrath. We are still susceptible to the wrath of both man and the Devil.

I have this final pertinent Bible verse for you: **'The servant is not greater than his Lord, if they have persecuted Me, they will also persecute you' (John 15:20).**

So get ready to endure war as it's coming, the other parts of my book about pestilence, famine and earthquake will be shortened somewhat. Then what I can include I will so that you can get prepared for them for your safety.

Byzantine

I remember from the streets that there is an old saying which says: 'What goes around, comes around'. I suppose that social justice would require that I stop right here to say that the Eastern Roman Empire (Byzantine) had slaves just as all Rome did. So when they were conquered by the Muslims of the Ottoman Turks they got sold into slavery themselves since that's what Muslims like to do.

If you remember I told you in a former chapter that Obama is not an Afro-American Christian but a Black African Muslim descendant from those same Black African Muslims who likewise sold their Black brothers into slavery, since that's what Muslims like to do.

I'm sure you remember how that Dr. Martin Luther King Jr. once had a dream that men would someday be judged by the content of their character and not the color of their skin. Obama was judged to be a good man because he is a semi-Black man. There are many Black Muslim inmates in the prisons and jails of America whose character leaves something to be desired, while Obama's character is at least questionable too as most of his crimes are still hidden.

The Bible says: **'There is nothing new under the sun that which is has already been done by them of old time' (Ecclesiastes 1:10).** In that light, threatened once Christian America needs to look at and carefully consider the Muslim conquest of Constantinople (the capitol of the Byzantine Empire) in 1453.

Before this Muslim conquest all of the cities that the Apostle John wrote to in his Revelation were beginning Christian. Now they are all part of the Muslim Caliphate of Turkey. Back then the Muslim Turks called themselves the Ottoman Empire. By eventually conquering Christian Constantinople, the Muslim Turks were now free to invade Europe.

As you know, many Muslim Turks today via lackadaisical immigration are continuing that invasion. In fact, in England today there are now more Mosques than Churches. Some experts even feel that England is rapidly becoming Muslim. Therefore this Muslim conquest of Christian Constantinople has dealt a massive blow to Christendom.

Beginning early in 1452 the young Sultan Mehmet II of the Ottoman Empire (he was just 19) built another fortress just North of Christian Constantinople. This was done to keep help from reaching Christian Constantinople. Since the Muslims owned most of the surrounding land, this just insured Christian Constantinople's encirclement.

Before the siege of Christian Constantinople began the Muslim Ottoman Empire had already developed the war weapon called the canon. About this same time an inventor (name: Urban) of a new larger size canon appeared on the scene. He tried to sell his new weapon of war to Constantine XI of the Byzantine Empire. But Constantine XI being advised by his passivist Holy Roman Christian subjects could not afford this new weapon. And would rather trust in God instead as Byzantine already had canons but not big enough for artillery.

So Urban sold his new larger style canon to the young Muslim Sultan instead. Urban's huge canon was named 'Basilica' for it was especially designed to destroy large Cathedrals, the largest stone buildings around. Plus it was 27 feet long and could hurl a 600 pound stone ball over a mile. Urban also stayed at the siege of Christian Constantinople in order to construct other canons and to advise how best to use them. The young Sultan, Mehmet II of the Ottoman Empire ordered his new canon to be put in place to begin the siege of Christian Constantinople.

<u>This one issue: having the most advanced military weapons available to defend your people rises again in this modern age.</u>

Some years ago the then President of the United States George H. W. Bush (Bush 41) was conned by America's pacifists to remove the neutron bomb from America's arsenal. Since that weapon was seen as an instigator of genocide, which the pacifists felt America should have nothing to do with.

If you remember this liar is the one who said: 'read my lips, no new taxes'. Then of course he raised taxes instead in order to fund America's liberal programs and entitlements.

United States President George W. Bush (Bush 43) having inherited the Bush family lying gene also said: 'We know there are weapons of mass destruction in Iraq'.

Now United States President George H. W. Bush (Bush 41)'s youngest son Jeb who also inherited that lying gene, lied about being Hispanic as he wants to make all America Hispanic too via amnesty for illegal immigrants.

Therefore with this atomic weapon removed from America's arsenal and with America's fear of using its remaining nuclear weapons it had no choice but to sacrifice its young men in hand to hand combat in the Iraq war. So today the male population of almost every town and city in America has much less men then woman. And some who did survive are now mentally and physically disabled. 1/6 of all American combat soldiers in that war now have PTSD.

The siege of Christian Constantinople took almost two months. During that time some Italian ships came to help Constantinople. But the Muslims sank them and captured their crews which they impaled on stakes in sight of the city's defenders. So in retaliation the Christian defenders of Constantinople brought forth their Ottoman prisoners and executed them publically for all to see.

During the siege of Christian Constantinople, since the canon breakthrough took so long other means were tried. Including one of digging tunnels to weaken the walls. The Ottoman Turks had two officers in charge of doing this who were seized by the Byzantines and tortured to reveal the location of all the Muslim tunnels. We may need to love our own enemies. But no scripture anywhere says to love the enemies of God.

<u>Here we see the need to use torture against God's enemies for the welfare and defense of your people contrary to what the pacifists say. And here we also see the need to execute promptly (without years of delay) and publically.</u>

Before I go on to reveal more truth about this conflict let me describe for you more about Byzantine, the Eastern Roman Empire.

The Eastern Roman Empire when it began controlled all the land from North Africa including Egypt across Palestine to modern day Turkey and Greece on North of Constantinople to the Slavic Regions. And Constantinople became literally the center of the Roman World. Its wall was built so strong and safe that the Muslim Ottoman Turks bypassed Constantinople at first to take more easy possession of lands lying to the North.

In time, the Byzantine Empire lost its land and became nothing more than a city state. Since I am not a historian, I will not go into the political and military reasons why it lost Egypt, Libya and Turkey.

But in considering once Christian America it has also lost some of its possessions, like those gained from the Spanish American War: both the Philippines and Cuba.

When I was a teenager I had to take the school bus to get to school. That bus usually picked me and others up about a quarter after seven in order to get us to school on time. If that bus was just a few minutes late I remember how we would have to wait at the railroad tracks for the long train to go by before we got to go.

Then obviously we'd be late for class. That long train that went by every morning before 7:30 was the army train. It had about five engines and almost 300 cars loaded with every form of military hardware, from jeeps and missiles to tanks with trucks armed with machine guns and recoilless rifles. The nation was getting ready for war; it was clear and obvious and scared some of us. Although the country prepared for the 'Bay of

Pigs' invasion of Cuba, such never materialized as president Kennedy was talked out of providing necessary air cover by the Democratic pacifists of that era. Thus this became just another 'rumor of war'.

Cuba was given its independence in 1926 and America had the right to take it back since it was being squandered on communism. But when America was well able to do so, it failed.

When a nation starts to lose its territory that's a very bad sign indeed and might help explain why Putin wants to expand Russia's influence over territory that it once ruled over.

There are several reasons why Constantinople (Byzantine) fell. I hope to cover them all here. One of the characteristics of the Byzantine Administration was its army of eunuchs that filled every post of every sort. These castrated people did not have balls enough to fight for their ideals, values and lands.

Likewise America today has too many gays draining the testosterone from men who can no longer fight for America's ideals, values and lands.

To Constantinople Persia was a continual malignant presence. Today just one of our enemies and the free world's is Iran, face it!

The Muslim Iran is the paragon of evil today seeking nuclear weapons to wipe Israel from the face of the earth. The Muslim advisor Valerie Jarrett is advising the Muslim Obama to agree with Muslim Iran over its gradual development of nuclear weapons to eliminate the Jewish state, because Muslims hate Jews.

Constantinople had 'Greek fire' (a weapon of fire used against wooden ships). Why didn't they develop that weapon to be used against men trying to climb up the walls of their city?

Likewise, America has nuclear weapons, how come one has not been developed into a tactical combat weapon instead of wasting the lives of thousands of our troops in hand to hand combat like in the Iraq War?

The Byzantine economic crisis was similar to America's own with both recession and inflation. Byzantine had gone from a mighty manufacturing and trading base to decline and eventual defeat. The Arabs (Muslim Turks) had brought out a new gold coin. Byzantine used its gold for icons instead.

Before its fall Constantinople (Byzantine) was also 'led from behind' as it was no longer able to dominate its neighbors or even influence other nations.

When Byzantine (Constantinople) did fall it was Serbia that stopped the Muslim advance into Europe. So when former president Clinton ordered Serbia to be bombed in favor of Bosnia and the Muslims gaining a foothold in Europe, he either showed himself to be a non-Christian or one with no sense of history.

Speaking of former President Bill Clinton it should be remembered how he continued the erosion of America's military might. First, America would no longer plan to win any nuclear exchange, but only to deter it. Second the US military will no longer plan to launch on warning but to absorb any first strike. Third many of America's bombers and missiles would be taken off alert status. By so doing this would ensure that America could not change its mind to get an attack off the ground even if a massive foreign (Russia, China or Pakistan) attack happened.

One of the main reasons why Constantinople or Byzantine was lost was because its defenders were so few while its enemies were so many. In that light, President Obama should be ashamed of himself for reducing America's army to the smallest armed force since 1940 and the Navy with the smallest number of warships since 1915. Someone needs to be elected who will see our defense as an entitlement to make America secure again. Not a chorus girl diplomatic appeaser like Hilary Clinton.

If you remember Hilary Clinton, then Obama's Secretary of State was the one who began this propaganda about the Arab Spring being the expansion of democracy. When she knew that it was the Muslim Obama's hidden desire to expand the Muslim Brotherhood instead.

In fact she knew that Obama is really a nominal Muslim by birth. He never was and is not now a real Christian. Nor was he ever converted from Islam to Christianity. She also knew that it was Obama's desire to cut back America's fortune so that Islam may triumph unchecked. And it was Obama's purpose to so promote the gay lifestyle and gay marriage as to emasculate America's armed forces.

There is another political problem here that needs to be exposed. Some feel that the US Constitution guarantees freedom of religion. Therefore both former president Bush and current demagogue Obama invited Muslims to settle in the country as if freedom of religion required such. But <u>Islam is not a religion of peace but, as history shows, a totalitarian ideology of conquest. Therefore the wholesale acceptance of Muslims into America should be stopped and those already here who have refused to assimilate into American society should be deported. We don't need the followers of false gods to contaminate our land.</u>

<u>California's problem with drought has more to do with political issues, like allowing Muslims to settle on their land and curse it by their presence on it then some foolish leftist notion like global warming. Also by diverting water from its farms to its cities to waste on illegal aliens calls for starving nations to sue California in the World Court (illegal aliens are not protected by citizenship and their needs do not outweigh the needs of millions of world citizens who need to eat).</u>

One very good point about Constantinople needs to be made here. Despite its many inadequacies and problems it had a state church. I know that the very idea of such horrifies most freedom loving Americans. But let's consider it closely. Constantinople was the capitol of the Eastern Roman Empire and all Romans were required to be Christian as part of their citizenship. There was no pluralistic pollution of many false gods in Constantinople.

One of the titles of the Emperor was 'defender of the faith'. So no ruler of the Byzantine Empire could be a non believer (like most modern politicians who lie about everything under the sun).

The other things that the Byzantine Empire (especially Constantinople) did not have were: no Mosques, no minarets and no Shari law. All law there was Roman.

Today America depends too much on Muslim lands (especially for oil to fuel our economy). It would be far better for America to become as self sufficient in oil as is possible. This means approve of oil drilling and its transport via pipelines.

As the siege was happening one day a soft, robbed dignitary of the Byzantine Empire (Constantinople) ventured to help defend the city at the huge wall. Unfortunately he was killed almost instantly. Panic set in as a hoard of Muslim Turks swarmed into the city. The shocked defenders ran for their Italian ships to escape but were struck down and beheaded by the Muslims.

Looking back on it all now, the Christian City fell primarily due to a lack of knowledge of God's word. Although the Byzantine Empire had a state church, their church controlled by priests did not teach its people to read the word of God for themselves. Even though most of the people were Greek and could read the Greek New Testament they failed to do so and let the priests handle the religious area of their lives.

The Bible says: **'God has not given us the spirit of fear but power, love and a sound mind' (I Timothy 1:7).** Such knowledge would have prevented panic. This clearly teaches the necessity of rescuing your old dusty Bible from its storage and reading its history and promises that could benefit you.

But Christianity is a Person, The Lord Jesus Christ, not just a teaching anyway. As it is written: **'He that has the Son has life and he that does not have the Son of God doesn't have that life (I John 5:12 of the Amplified Bible).**

Once one repents of their sins, takes Jesus into their heart and becomes a real Christian they have only gained first base in the game of life. If they hit against evil, they may gain another base or two (sanctification). But if one preservers to obtain Holy Spirit Baptism then they cross home plate and score a run.

Then the love of God is shed abroad in their heart by the Holy Spirit. But the world has not yet seen real love, the love of God used as a weapon.

We Christians have seen the love of God mistakenly wasted on infidels (Muslims) who do not properly respect the Lord Jesus Christ as the Son of God.

Some time ago two modern Christian miracle workers (faith healers) went to work miracles in Muslim lands. They were: Leif Hetland who went to Pakistan and Benny Hinn who went to Indonesia. Both of these Spirit filled Christians held healing crusades and many Muslims were healed. Most Christians rejoice over the healings because they have the typical American middleclass mindset that the end justifies the means.

However Muslims believe differently about Jesus then Christians do. In fact they believe that their false god Allah sent Jesus in answer to their prayers to him. <u>No false god tells Jesus what to do or orders Him around.</u> Next, I'll include for your benefit a whole chapter on the Muslim Jesus so that you will be able to see what I mean.

But since such love as a weapon requires so much personal spirituality that does not come through the preaching of either the pre-tribulation rapture or prosperity maybe it would be easier for Christians to adequately arm themselves to fight fire with fire. In that regard my following chapters may give some insight.

It should be remembered that the Muslim Ottoman Turks were the socialists (Nazis) of their day. Like ISIS now they provided public social service including public education and a primitive form of Health Care (public baths) that was used to help counter act the Black Death Plague back then.

It may come as a shock to many but Obama Care doesn't just come from socialism but from Muslim socialism an integral part of Obama's personal Muslim nature.

Thanks to Obama, the graduate universities of America are now overflowing with Muslim students from all over the world who get to rip off White Christian America by claiming minority status and by getting IRS tax refunds for supposedly overpaying taxes to get their advanced public education entitlement at taxpayer's expense while America's infrastructure deteriorates and crumbles into disrepair while millions of Americans both White and Black remain out of work. And how can real native born Americans find work if millions of illegal immigrants get what few jobs remain?

In fact, just like the Muslim Ottoman Turks, Obama now plans to rip off White Christian America to pay for all his entitlements and stupid social policies benefiting Black Muslim immigrants and their Black Muslim converts. Thus Muslim immigrant expansions into our Black communities have now poisoned race relations in America and setup our next civil war. And illegal immigration and continued 'sell out' trade agreements have deprived the American people of jobs and hurt their current financial well being to such an extent that they'll be needing to get even too.

After these Muslim problems gets resolved and after the coming civil war, more tribulation will come. In the New Testament of the Bible, Matthew 24:6 the promise of wars to come is plural. (wars is plural).

Muslims are just deceived men. They are not supernatural. Their prophet Mohamed is a false prophet. And their god: Allah is also false. So don't fear them.

The supernatural army that's coming is described in the first few verses of Revelation, chapter nine. The King James version describes these enemies from hell as locusts. But actually ancient American Indian tribes and other pre-flood peoples painted pictures of these creatures in their caves. And these creatures look reptilian and they killed off whatever giants survived the flood. Then they went back to hell to await the time of their coming release again to kill evil mankind. Their image is confirmed by modern experts into extra terrestrial aliens heard over coasttocoastam.com radio.

In any case there is a confirmed portal to the underworld, outerspace and other dimensions of time used for research into the future by the Roman Catholic Church at the Mount Graham Observatory in Arizona.

These creatures are real, the Bible says so and they are coming your way unless you forsake your sins and accept Christ. Then this judgment could pass over us entirely and visit another generation more sinful and evil than ourselves.

The American Civil War

From the definition of wars we already expect wars to be between Nations and Kingdoms. The Geneva Convention recognizes nations at war as those sovereign states that are recognized by or are members of the United Nations. Whereas back in Jesus day kingdoms were simple city states ruled over by a local king. The size of the nation or the kingdom may vary but war was an official conflict between them.

A nation may be limited or defined by common language, common religion or recognized political boundaries. Some nations may have different economies and different types of governments. But all are capable of war. And apparently that's what these few phrases in **Matthew 24: verse7** indicated. In fact war is a universal condition common to all political entities. And war comes to all just like changes in the weather.

Some wars are called civil wars when in reality they are an independent branch of the whole, fighting against the whole for differences in belief based on economy, theology or politics. The American Civil War is a good example.

In any war usually those who win the war write the history of it that is approved to be taught in school. **But here through God's prophetic gifting we get to say some truthful things that need to be said.**

Those engaged in this war wanted to be gentlemen and show forth from their manners that they were raised well. As in the first battle of the American Civil War, which the Confederates won. Stonewall Jackson exercising gentlemanly civility and respect asked Jefferson Davis if it was alright for him to go on to take Washington. Jefferson Davis wanting to show civilian control of the military, said no. Stonewall Jackson should have kept his mouth shut. Since when you're winning you don't ask someone else how far you should go. If Stonewall Jackson, the soldier, had moved against Washington he could have easily taken it, burned it to the ground and hung Lincoln in the front yard of the White House. If this had happened, just think what a different country

America would be today. There would not now be any American welfare state with trillions of dollars in debt to maintain social programs that our children must pay for instead of being able to live their own lives.

Remember when you were a child and used to play games with other kids. If another kid was wrong about something and exhibited bad behavior toward you, like stealing your marbles or spitting on your cards, you gathered up your stuff and went home. Well, that's just what happened at the start of the Civil War. The pious North began playing hardball with the Southerners over the issue of extending slavery into the territories. So the South said we're keeping our economic system and went home (withdrew from the union by succession). But after they left, the North refused to also leave and still kept Fort Sumter in Charleston harbor, South Carolina, Confederate States of America and refused to vacate so after some reasonable time, the South opened fire.

This same problem also exists today. America has been warned repeatedly to get out of Japan, Germany, Korea and now many Muslim lands but refuses to do so. Such invites tragedy and causes outlandish expense being passed on to our children in the form of deficit spending.

Expect: more government deficit spending even on wars on credit.

At the beginning of the Civil War many commissioned officers felt that this was just a dispute and not worthy of total war. President Lincoln went through many gentleman generals until he found a few savage rouges (drunks) in uniform that would do Lincoln's bidding.

One took Richmond, the other burned Atlanta to the ground. Their underlings also in uniform killed all the farm animals and every horse in order to keep the occupants of these Southern cities confined there to starve to death. This war crime was Lincoln's **'charity to all and malice toward none'**.

154

Blacks had much more under slavery than they wound up with thanks to these 'Northern liberators'. For example; under slavery, Blacks had a job for life that they could not be fired from. Now they have unemployment and unemployment compensation thanks to your increased taxes. Under slavery

Blacks also lived in the country with clean air and water and freedom from crime. Now they live in filthy Black ghettos like Chicago where people are killed every night.

The Blacks were also promised by the North 40 acres and a mule to encourage a slave rebellion. Of course the North never divided up any plantations in order to fulfill this promise but instead Northern armies pillaged slave cabins and stole from the civilian population both Black and White, which is another war crime.

Maybe there is still one truth about this war that made it into a few history books anyway. That is how Lincoln threatened and abused with military action the state legislature of Maryland in order to keep them from also voting for succession just like the rest of the South.

The Bible says that there is nothing new under the sun (Ecclesiastes 1:9). Many real patriots resent the Patriot ACT and the loss of liberty imposed recently on us by George Bush 43. Actually Lincoln had a similar modus operandi plus Lincoln also had people held without trial and in many cases without charge. The conditions of the prisons that Lincoln used would also be considered a war crime today.

Lincoln was a very mean and ruthless man. Much of his anger was caused at the beginning of the war by the unfortunate shooting of his pet homosexual lover in Virginia when that young man went to take down the confederate flag flying in Virginia which Lincoln had to see every day. Yes, the high voiced Lincoln was also a known Sodomite. That's what they called gays back in those days.

The book: <u>THE INTIMATE WORLD of ABRAHAM LINCOLN</u> BY Professor and sex researcher of Alfred Kinsey fame Dr. C.A. Tripp reveals on page XVII of its introduction that there were at least five verifiable cases of President Abraham Lincoln's sexual activity with other men, although you never heard anything about them when we studied American History in school.

As you know the Bible has been taken out of school, but it still says in Numbers 32:23 'Be sure your sin will find you out'. And the Lord Jesus said in Luke 12:2 'for there is nothing covered that shall not be revealed, neither hid that shall not be known'.

<u>Your Bible is your guidebook to keep you free from sin. Study it!</u>

In that light the last one, and certainly the most famous one was the relationship President Abraham Lincoln had with Captain David V. Derickson during The Civil War, of whom Lincoln said; 'The Captain and I are getting quit thick'.

The Captain, David V. Derickson, was a forty-four year old (grown man which makes him a consenting adult) Buck tail soldier from Pennsylvania. He was five feet nine inches tall; with intense eyes, a strong nose and thick black hair from a socially prominent family in Meadville, Pennsylvania and was assigned to be Lincoln's bodyguard.

Of Derickson sleeping in the same bed with Lincoln Virginia Woodbury Fox noted in her detailed diary, in an entry dated November 16, 1862, "there is a Buck tail soldier here devoted to the President, drives with him, and when Mrs. L. is not home sleeps with him. What stuff!"

Margaret Leech in her book entitled; <u>Reveille in Washington, 1860-1865</u> mentions this man on page 303 in which she states: "Lincoln grew to like the Buck tails, especially company K, with whose Captain he became so friendly that he invited him to share his bed on autumn nights when Mrs. Lincoln was away from home".

Also in a detailed history entitled; <u>History Of The One Hundred And Fiftieth Regiment, Pennsylvania Volunteers, Second Regiment, Buck tail Brigade,</u> Published in 1895 written by Lieutenant Colonel Chamberlain, the immediate commanding officer of Captain Derickson, states in chapter four of his book that; "the President was also not an infrequent visitor in the late afternoon, and had endeared himself to his guards by his genial, kind words. He was not long at placing officers in his two companies at their ease in his presence, and Captains Derickson and Crozier where shortly on a footing of such marked friendship with him that they were often summoned to dinner or breakfast at the Presidential board. Captain Derickson, in particular, advanced so far in the President's confidence and his esteem that in Mrs. Lincoln's absence he frequently spent the night at his cottage, sleeping in the same bed with him, and – it is said – making use of his Excellency's nightshirt! Thus began an intimacy which continued unbroken until the following spring, when Captain Derickson was appointed provost marshal of the Nineteenth Pennsylvania District with headquarters in Meadville".

Finally in the book; <u>Lincoln Day By Day: A Chronology 1809 to 1865</u>. It is recorded that Mrs. Lincoln left the White House to shop and visit friends both in New York and Boston. She left on October 25th 1862. She returned on November 27th. The entry Virginia Fox made in her diary about the Buck tail soldier sleeping in the same bed with Lincoln falls during this time.

So the fact that Abraham Lincoln had bed time partners or sexual partners other than his wife, who were even male, is now well documented and clear for all to see. The Lincoln bed is still famous for lust even today. So much so that former President Bill Clinton used to rent it out.

Lincoln's fraudulent sexual orientation has already been examined, but since this book is neither a sex research work nor a political attack something else lies behind Lincoln's devious sex life that is far more important for us to consider now, and that something is **<u>Sovereignty.</u>**

Although Abraham Lincoln was elected with just forty percent of the popular vote, he still considered himself to be the elected **Sovereign** of the U. S. much like President Bush who only won by a few votes yet considers himself to have won a mandate complete with political capitol to do as he pleases with your tax dollars and the lives of your children wasted in a stupid anti-Muslim Iraq war. While at the same time allowing Muslim 'interpreters' to settle in America to curse our land.

Being an elected **Sovereign** did not make Lincoln any less of a **Sovereign**, he can still rule just as constitutional monarchs do, and even without any constitutional restraints if at war, for then he had 'war powers'. But starting a war, like the Civil War, without the consent of Congress in Vallandigham's opinion; "would have cost any English **Sovereign** his head at any time within the last two hundred years".

Common practice in that day for the various **Sovereigns** of Europe was to sleep with their bodyguards, especially if at war. **Sovereigns** could have any type of sex that they wanted at any time with anyone, 'Devine Right of Kings'. Usually their bedmates were also their sexual playmates.

In America, the true image of a **Sovereign** is not fully grasped. A **Sovereign** usually has absolute power to do as they please. That includes being above the law, as The Indemnity Act of 1863 provided. That act insulated Lincoln, the Lincoln Administration and all federal government officials from being sued in any state court.

Sovereigns could also act as they please where sex was concerned. In the Middle Ages in Europe, **Sovereigns** had not only harems of women, but also those of young boys. In fact, Pope Innocent III had eight boys to bed down with. At that time, having sex was expected by those in high office and was usually lavished upon them. It was just another one of the entitlements that usually came with the job of high office especially under the spoils system where anything goes.

Contrary to public opinion, entitlements did not begin with the Democrats or Democratic President Franklin Roosevelt, or his 'New Deal', or with Social Security's cost of living. **Entitlements began with <u>Sovereignty</u> and with the Republican President Abraham Lincoln, 'The Magnificent'.** For a man like Lincoln, without Christian inhibitions, to be sexually starved at first just resulted in frustration. But as time went on, his frustration became fury, since as a Sovereign, having sex was his due.

<u>Expect: someone else's entitlement may cause you to do without. So get your stuff NOW!</u>

You might remember how that another Republican President, Richard Nixon, when denied having marital sex during the Vietnam War got hostile and secretly bombed Cambodia, which he denied in public. Likewise, Republican President Lincoln, also full of testosterone sent General Sheridan to waste the Shenandoah Valley and General Sherman to burn Atlanta.

General Sheridan was told by General Grant, whose portrait appears on your fifty dollar bill, "to make another trip down the valley, pillaging, plundering and burning everything in sight. Carry off stock of all descriptions and Negroes, so as to prevent further planting". Thus the Shenandoah Valley was to become so devastated that "crows flying over it would need to pack their own lunches". It was thus turned into a desert and its residents rendered homeless.

Lincoln thanked Sheridan's Army for doing this in this way since he believed that 'might makes right' and he could ignore the Constitution, the Geneva Convention and even common decency and morality as long as his military won. If Lincoln lost, he knew that he and his top generals would be hung as war criminals, because that's just what they were!

<u>Expect: any war to be a total war that will either hurt or kill you.</u>

His top Generals; Grant, Sheridan, and Sherman all followed his lead, and obeyed his orders as soldiers always do. Their objective was to totally destroy the Southern economy and starve out its civilian population as much as possible to end once and for all **states' rights <u>Sovereignty</u>**, not to free the slaves, which was merely a cover.

Many slaves who ended up in the hands of the Union army were not set free despite the Emancipation Proclamation, but were put to work doing the most unpleasant work in and around army encampments. In short, Lincoln's Emancipation Proclamation was only applied to rebel territory. Some States like Maryland, Kentucky, and West Virginia were specifically exempted.

Lincoln, one of the nation's preeminent lawyers, an obviously trained liar and master of deceit was careful to so craft his Emancipation Proclamation in such an arbitrary way as to please the abolitionist without really freeing a single slave.

Lincoln maintained that his Emancipation Proclamation was just 'a war power' that he had the power to declare since the U.S. was at war. <u>In reality, the President had no such power at that time to dictate such to any state.</u> Today of course presidents routinely dictate thousands of laws, regulations and executive orders that they also fail to fund to every state and local government. It was the Republican President Abraham Lincoln who started this.

<u>Expect: unfunded executive orders that will cost you dearly.</u>

Most people of the North in 1863 were shocked and surprised by the Emancipation Proclamation for they had not been told by either the U. S. government or the Lincoln Administration that they were fighting and dying by the thousands for the well being of slaves in far away states most northerners had never been to and had never seen. **Hostile White immigrant mobs had assaulted Blacks in northern cities for years,**

so in July 1863 there were race riots in New York City as Whites protested both the Emancipation Proclamation and Lincoln's new conscription law.

Expect: race riots so be sure you live in an area that is at least 90% your own race to avoid racial conflict, or to be safe move to a place that is.

This conscription law applied only to Whites, but those with sufficient funds could buy their way out of this draft for three hundred dollars. Those without this money were outraged and the resulting rioting mob consisted of these defrauded people. Instead of even attempting to reason with these people, Lincoln immediately sent five regiments of battle hardened troops from the recently concluded Battle of Gettysburg to New York City to quell the riots. These battle-hardened troops achieved their goal of quelling the riots by shooting and killing over three hundred protestors and using their bayonets to disperse the crowds of protestors.

At this time the mayhem in New York City was atrocious. The streetlights were out, many hangings and murders occurred as terror and anxiety was common. All the shops were closed and business was at a standstill. All carriages and buses had ceased running. Telegraph wires were cut, and even railroad tracks were torn up. No Black person dared to show themselves on that day. Colored people weren't even safe in their own homes.

Expect: Mayhem so move to a safe place NOW!

The very idea that the Civil War happened because the people in the North adopted abolitionist feelings and were morally constrained to free the slaves is obviously fraudulent. For no abolitionist was ever elected to any major political office in any Northern state. The overwhelming majority of White Northerners cared little if at all about the welfare of slaves and treated Blacks that

lived among them with contempt, ridicule, discrimination, and even violence.

The author Eugene Berwanger described the condition of Blacks in the North at this time in his book: <u>North of Slavery</u>. He writes: **"In virtually every phase of existence (In the North), Negroes found themselves systematically separated from Whites. They were either excluded from railway cars, omnibuses stage coaches, and steam boats or assigned to special 'Jim Crow' sections; they sat, when permitted, in secluded and removed corners of theaters and lecture halls; they could not enter most hotels, restaurants, and resorts, except as servants: they prayed in 'Negro pews' in the White churches, and if partaking of the Sacrament of the Lord's Supper, they waited until the Whites had been served the bread and wine. Moreover, they were often educated in segregated schools, punished in segregated prisons, nursed in segregated hospitals and buried in segregated cemeteries".**

In addition to these riots, the Emancipation Proclamation also caused a desertion crisis in the U. S. army. At least two hundred thousand federal soldiers deserted; another one hundred and twenty thousand avoided conscription by fleeing to Canada or hiding out in the mountains, just like during the Vietnam War, a hundred years later.

History also records that the Emancipation Proclamation then, just like the Iraq War now also caused an enlistment shortfall in the US Army. Many soldiers said that they felt betrayed as they were willing to risk their lives for the Union but not for Black freedom from slavery. Likewise today Americans are willing to defend America, but not die for Iraq's democracy or that some Muslim girl can get an education.

Lincoln failed to take the common practice every other nation employed during this time where slavery was ended peacefully and even compensated for. Lincoln maintained that he was not particularly supportive of emancipation. He viewed it as only a tool to be used by him to deceive in order to achieve his real objective: **the consolidation of all state power in him, the elected <u>Sovereign.</u>**

By this time, Sherman's Army had become extremely adept at pillage and plunder. His Army was composed of both big city criminals and foreign convicts fresh from the jails of Europe. Somewhat like Fidel Castro's dumping on America of his 'low life scum' from his jails during the Muriel boat lift.

Additionally, history records that the federal soldiers routinely robbed everyone at gunpoint and in broad daylight during the mayhem of the Civil War.

<u>Expect robbery by government official's not just gangs.</u>

In those days, federal soldiers under Sherman sacked after plundering the finest Southern Plantations then **proceeded to do likewise to the lowest slave cabins.**

Mark Grimsley records in his book: <u>The Hard Hand of War: Union Military Policy</u> <u>toward Southern Civilians, 1861-1865</u> 'with the utter disregard for Blacks that was the norm among Union Troops, that the soldiers ramshackled the slave cabins, taking whatever they liked'. Many accounts also record that Black woman (who were often gang raped by Union troops) suffered the most and that many Black men as a result hated the Union Armies. (The University of South Carolina has diaries, which record many rapes of Black woman right out in the public in broad daylight as if they had been caught like farm animals in heat ready to be exploited).

<u>EXPECT Rape.</u>

Emancipation was a farce, which the Blacks could see through. For they lost not only their jobs with whatever benefits they may have earned but also their homes. In those days, a slave usually got good health care along

with free housing as owners 'property care'. Once Lincoln forced his will upon the South, the Blacks were free from any job, any place to stay or any care except Government care. <u>This is where unemployment and government handouts like welfare came from.</u>

<u>Expect unemployment.</u>

Sherman's Army also killed many thousands upon thousands of horses, cattle, hogs, dogs, and every domestic animal in sight so that the Southerners would starve.

The Geneva Convention of 1863 said that any naval blockade is an act of war upon a country's civilian population as well as its armed forces. The nations of the civilized world also agreed then that it was a war crime, punishable by either death or imprisonment for armies to: (1) Attack defenseless cities and towns, (2) Plunder and destroy civilian property, (3) Take from the civilian population more than what is necessary to feed any occupying army. They also had concluded that the only just war was a defensive war. On this count alone Lincoln's invasion of the South made him a war criminal, not a hero worthy of a memorial in his honor. Moreover occupying soldiers who destroy private property, farms and houses are to be called 'Savage Barbarians' not national heroes.

<u>Expect: Unconventional, uncivilized, non-Geneva Convention, barbaric war.</u>

<u>Lincoln wanted Southern civilians to suffer.</u> This required him to abandon the Geneva Convention. Republican President Bush has now followed suit in order to make the 'terrorist Iraqi' suffer without any Geneva Convention rights. This abuse comes from the Civil War, known as Lincoln's 'total war'. And it was such waged against innocent, non-combatant civilians, mostly woman, children, and old men, and not a regular army. Now if these victims of 'total war' should survive enough to fight back

they are called insurgences. Back then they were called gorillas. And innocent civilian had to pay with either their lives or their houses burnt along with their crops destroyed for whatever harm was inflicted by the Confederates upon the Union Forces.

Before reaching Atlanta, Sherman's army had already abused much of the South. Sherman described what his army had done as they passed through Meridian, Mississippi. He reported; "for five days, ten thousand, worked hard and with a will, in that work of destruction, with axes, sledges, crowbars, claw bars, and with fire, and I have no hesitation in pronouncing the work well done. Meridian . . . no longer exists".

The first major battle of the Civil War was fought in Manassas, Virginia, on July 16, 1861. The Union Army of General Erwin McDowell had amassed some thirty-three thousand troops to attack twenty-two thousand Confederate troops only thirty miles west of Washington. DC. There was great optimism especially in Washington that the Civil War would end that day. Many locals from Washington road out to Manassas Junction in their carriages with their packed lunches in hopes of watching the Confederates soon and certain surrender. But it didn't turn out that way, for the battle was a resounding Confederate victory. In fact, the battle ended with a wild scramble of mob force of defeated Union Troops and shocked civilians retreating back to Washington. This whole mob was several miles long and a few football field lengths wide composed of wild-eyed survivors running for their lives, hoping to find shelter in Washington.

It was here that General Jackson earned his nickname by furiously turning back and defeating decisively an overpowering Union Force. After the battle, he approached the Confederate President, Jefferson Davis, whom he saw on the battlefield and said to him; "give me ten thousand men and I will take Washington tomorrow". Davis being the gentleman, refused. He later said that he regretted that decision for the rest of his life and considered it to be **'one of the greatest mistakes of the war'**.

The Confederates made many other mistakes too, which cost them the war. They were too honorable, so they refused to assassinate Lincoln even though they knew that he traveled without an armed escort from Washington to the Presidential retreat in the Maryland Mountains. They could also have used landmines at their boarders to keep Lincoln's invaders out, but they failed to grasp that their disagreements with the Union had now degenerated into Lincoln's 'total war' which at first they failed to recognize, and did not desire to wage.

So gentlemanly conduct on the part of the South probably cost them the first Civil War. The fluoridation of municipal tap water across America may cost you Christians the next Civil War.

On a recent radio talk show Ty Bollinger was discussing his new book about his cancer research entitled: <u>Cancer: Step Outside the Box.</u> In his interview he mentioned how that many contaminants now in our society are causing an increase in cancer. One of these contaminants is fluoride.

Fluoride was first developed in the Nazi death camps during World War II to remove ones will to fight so that the unfortunate inmates would remain docile and apathetic until their eventual execution. Back then the Americans classified fluoride as a rat poison for civilian use not as a chemical weapon in war.

Today fluoride is used in almost all municipal tap water systems across America. Besides rendering the population docile, this chemical also has a very interesting side effect.

Apparently fluoride also increases the estrogen level and helps decrease the testosterone level of those who ingest it. In other words, this fluoridation of public drinking water is responsible for feminizing the population (increasing breast and other female cancers). This is also seen visibly in the increase of the gay population, with normal men becoming gay and indulging in Gay marriage. Thus the gay lifestyle results from chemical poisoning moreso than from just being born that way.

After all General Sherman's War Crimes were reported to Lincoln, Lincoln said that this was exactly the type of war that he wanted waged against the South. Whereupon he promptly awarded General Sherman and told him to proceed to Georgia, and especially to Atlanta to 'steal his further reward'.

After likewise abusing the outskirts of Atlanta, Georgia, General Sherman entered the city, the city of Atlanta was then bombed night and day until barely a building survived. After destroying much of the city, General Sherman's army then looted and burned whatever remained. Even the cemeteries were looted, with graves being dug up and cadavers stripped of their jewelry and valuables especially including any gold, like gold pocket watches and gold teeth, just like the Nazi's did in another war complete with war crimes some eighty years later.

There were approximately four thousand homes in Atlanta before the bombardment started; afterward only four hundred were left standing. More than ninety percent of the city of Atlanta was totally destroyed and its churches were demolished too.

Once in Atlanta, Sherman decided to depopulate the city and he ordered everyone out with whatever belongings that they could carry. Those so ordered were the civilian inhabitants of the city, thousands of woman, children, and old men. Those who couldn't or wouldn't leave were first rendered homeless as their homes were burnt, and if they still refused to vacate, then they were shot. There was so much blood from the many bodies of Atlanta, Georgia that the name of the Chattahoochee River was recommended to be changed to the Crimson River.

One diary of Sherman's soldiers was found to document what happened when Sherman was still in Atlanta. It records: "never before have I witnessed so much wanton destruction as on this march. This was indeed an ogre of robbing, plundering, and then burning. The soldiers acted as if they had become drunken brut beasts on a rampage". Another Union soldier recorded that "he doubted that there was a single virgin in the whole army with all the homeless black woman needing to be rescued from the streets of Atlanta".

As Sherman's army left Atlanta burning, they trampled down the local farm fields so that no crops for food could reach those in Atlanta. The streets of Atlanta were filled with the rotting carcasses of horses, hogs and cattle that the invaders shot to keep those who survived the burning of Atlanta from eating. Since people will not eat from rotting carcasses it was believed that this practice would bring about the starvation of whomever in Atlanta survived the burning.

At this time, a Mrs. Walton wrote her description of this event to her daughter. She wrote, "The Yankees broke up and split up two of my bureau drawers, split up one of my secretary drawers, they broke up and opened one of your bundles I don't know what was in it, took things. They took all my meat, sugar, coffee, flour, the knives and forks, the spoons and all they could get into...They then broke up my caster, carried off the pepper box top, stomped the caster and broke it. Tell Mary that they took the Amber type she gave me of Joe's. They took all my corn, hogs, killed the goats, took chickens, broke open every trunk I had in the house...They took my home spun dress and one smarter one, Took all my shoes and stockings, my scarf and the silk that was left of my dress. They got my needles, thimble, scissors, and thread". But much of this and other plunder was usually abandoned at the Yankee campsite since it impeded the Union army in waging more destruction on their way through The South. It should also be noted that **they did not steel out of any need, but simply out of greed and pure meanness.**

Sherman's Army, after destroying Atlanta made a swath of destruction through the rest of Georgia all the way to the sea. From there they went into South Carolina, the birthplace of the Confederacy. Here they continued pillaging, plundering, and sacking every inhabited community as they had just done in Georgia. As they entered South Carolina, it seems that an intoxication of enraged fury overcame them. This intoxication intensified as the Union Army neared Columbia, the state capitol.

A Major Connolly in Sherman's Army wrote to his wife that: "the army burned everything it came near in the state of South Carolina". Another one of Sherman's officers said; "A majority of these cities, towns, villages, and country houses have been burnt to the ground".

It should be noted that, at this time, the slaves suffered too. Slaves were frequently ordered on pain of death to disclose where their master had hid his valuables. Once these valuables were found, they were destroyed right in front of the slaves and the plantation was looted and then destroyed and burned. As a result, hundreds of half starved Blacks who were already psychologically damaged by 'shell shock' had to follow Sherman's army to eat whatever they could find that was still edible. **To get rid of these 'low life scavengers', when ever Sherman's army came to a river or stream that they had to cross, first after his army built a bridge of pontoons they would cross over them, then they dismantled the pontoons and removed them before the Blacks had a chance to follow. (Since Blacks could not swim and feared the water they had to stay in the South and starve and could not migrate North).**

Here is a personal testimony of the aftermath of Sherman's army of destruction as recorded in the diary of one Miss Andrews: "about three miles from Sparta we struck the burnt country, as it is well named by the natives, and then I could better understand the wrath and desperation of these poor people. There was hardly a fence left standing all the way from Sparta to Gordon. The fields were trampled down and the road was lined with the carcasses of horses, hogs, and cattle that the invaders either unable to consume or to carry away with them, had wantonly shot to starve out the people and prevent them from eating and making the crops. The stench in some places was unbearable. The dwellings that were standing all showed signs of pillage, and on every plantation we saw the charred remains of the cotton gin house and pat can screw, where here and there lone chimney stacks, 'Sherman's sentinels', told of homes laid in ashes". Was this not the typical terrorist assault of what was to become known as "Total War"?

Once Sherman's army did enter Columbia, South Carolina after burning every town on the way, the diary of one eighteen year old survivor named Emma LeConte described what happened. According to her; "Sherman's army was well equipped with matches, crow bars, and other tools of the arsonist and plunderer". She wrote, "as soon as the bulk of the army entered the work of pillage began". The city was literally destroyed right before her eyes. She went on to describe how the Union soldiers, men dressed in uniform, acted like criminal arsonists. "They would enter a house and in the presence of helpless woman and children pour turpentine on their beds and set them on fire. When the women and some old men tried to put out the fire with fire hoses, soldiers armed with bayonets would cut through the fire hoses to ensure that the fire burned all the way to the ground ".

She further wrote: "imagine a night turned into noonday, only with a blazing scorching glare that was horrible – a copper colored sky across which swept columns of black, rolling, smoke glittering with sparks and foam embers, while all around us were falling thickly showers of burning flakes. Everywhere the palpitating blaze walling the streets with solid masses of flames as far as the eye could reach, filling the air with its horrible roar. On every side the racking and devouring fire, while every instant came the crashing timbers of thunder of falling buildings. A quivering molten ocean seems to fill the air and sky. The Library building opposite us seemed framed by the gushing flames and smoke, while through the windows gleamed the liquid fire".

She further described those soldiers as being "infuriated, cursing, screaming, exalting in their work".

She concluded that she did not believe that any house had escaped pillage. She said of the houses throughout the city of Columbia, "those that the flames sparred were entered by brutal soldiery and everything wantonly destroyed".

After his march of destruction Sherman met with both Lincoln and Grant at City Point on the James River on March 27, 1865 where he described his exploits of evil. Sherman described all about his marches to both Lincoln and Grant. Sherman's personal memoirs also record that Lincoln particularly enjoyed hearing about the mayhem of the bummers as looters were called back then.

When I was in high school we studied American history. Of course back then in my youth, none of these truths were ever revealed, even though I went to school in a southern state. Some historians now claim that Lincoln had no knowledge of these events and did not order Sherman's destruction of the South. Those who make such claims fail to face the recorded facts of history and to acknowledge even the simple military chain of command. Sherman was not on his own to do his own thing as he pleased. But was a soldier under orders to abolish the Southern economic system in order to both starve out the secessionists and **to stamp out once and for all, states' rights Sovereignty.**

Even if somehow it came to light that Lincoln's exact orders did not bring about all this destruction, nevertheless Lincoln's recorded meeting with Sherman on March 27, 1865 documents for history both his approval and gratitude for what the terrorist Sherman had done to the South.

British military historian B.H.L. Hart wrote that: 'Lincoln's policy was in many ways the prototype of modern total war, for it employed terrorism against innocent, non-combative, civilians and the destruction of civil life in the South. This policy broke the code of civilized warfare as it inflicted suffering on innocence not on armed soldiers in a conflict of war'.

As I have shown and as the historical facts confirm both generals Sheridan and Sherman were in effect terrorists of their day for they not only burnt civilians alive, both also slaughtered farm animals burnt barns and crops and looted and torched cities. They made their destructive abuses and war crimes against humanity into legitimate acts of war.

Expect: War Crimes to become legitimate acts of war.

Later on when the U.S. had trouble with the plains Indians, Sherman who had burned Atlanta said; 'We must act with vindictive earnestness against the Sioux, even to their extermination, men, women and children'. Sheridan having also learned 'total war' said, 'the only good Indians I ever saw were dead'. Sherman not wanting to be clipped called for the massacre of all American Indians as the 'final solution to the Indian problem'. As you know this same term; 'Final Solution' was also used by another terrorist government (Nazis) in another war some eighty years later.

Being fair here, the Nazis were not the only ones to employ terror. During the Second World War, in February, 1945 the alias fire bombed Dresden and killed hundreds of thousands of desperate civilian refugees fleeing the Soviet Army. The Washington Post wrote on its fiftieth anniversary that; "If any one person can be blamed for the tragedy of Dresden, it appears to have been Churchill'. Before leaving Yalta, Churchill had ordered Allied Air Power to 'de-house' German civilians to make them into refugees clogging the roads over which German soldiers had to move to fight off the Red Army's winter offensive".

This mission of terror involved 770 Lancaster bombers that dropped 650,000 incinerary bombs on Dresden with 1,474 tons of high explosives. Then five hundred American B17's also helped to bomb that city into the Stone Age. The fires thus ignited burned for seven days and melted the streets. Those attempting to flee got their shoes burned off and feet scorched. Thousands who sought refuge in their cellars, died there, as they were starved for the oxygen that the flames devoured, then their buildings collapsed upon them, thus they became entombed.

Once this terror begins in the Civil War it continued on to where General Curtis LeMay's forces of B 29's bombed Tokyo. One describes it as; "On March 9, 1945, 179 American bombers, armed with incinerary bombs intended to torch the wood and paper Japanese Capitol appeared over Tokyo, a city with a population density of one hundred and thirty five thousand per square mile. All went according to plan. Tokyo was consumed by fire so ferocious that the heat boiled the water in the lakes and ponds, cooking those who fled to safety there like human lobsters".

Six months later Truman dropped the Atom bomb on both Hiroshima and Nagasaki blotting out the lives of hundreds of thousands of civilians instantly. "If war terror is the deliberate slaughter of non combatants, to break the will of the enemy, were not Dresden, Tokyo, Hiroshima and Nagasaki war terror on a monumental scale?"

While we condemn terror, it succeeds and will be employed again and again to achieve goals worth dying for. Generals Sherman and Sheridan had the Union armies crush and destroy the South so as to set it back a hundred years.

Expect: Terrorism.

In modern times, the IRA, the Stern Gang, the FLN, the Mau Mau, the Irgun, the ANC, the Viet Minh all used terror to change history. The innocent blood shed in revolutions that succeeded was quickly washed away by victory.

Terrorism often succeeded in the twentieth century, and when it did, the ex-terrorist achieved political power, glory, and immortality, with streets, towns, and cities named for them. And today America recognizes every one of these regimes that came out of wars where terrorism was used. For example, today

Saigon, once the capitol of South Vietnam is now called Ho Chi Minh City.

'One man's terrorist is another man's freedom fighter'. Nations, empires, ethnic groups, republics, monarchs, dictators, rebels, revolutionaries, and anarchists have all used terror to win their respective wars including consolidating their tyranny, expelling colonial powers and achieving the national independence of their cause.

So then Bush's "War on Terrorism" is just a propaganda fraud of getting the American people to pay his Iraq war debt for foolish political pork barrel projects, like the rebuilding of Iraq so that the American people can no longer afford their domestic social programs that they now need big time.

"Modernity often forgives the sins of terrorists because of the nobility of the cause they served". For example, today both Generals Sheridan and Sherman are forgiven because they supposedly freed the slaves. But today the Blacks are not yet free of poverty, police brutality or other miscarriages of justice. True, they are now free of their masters, his housing, and his 'property care'. In other words, now they have neither jobs nor a place to stay with food to eat and provided health care or other benefits. So just how much good did the terrorism known as The Civil War really accomplish for anybody's good?

Let me conclude this section on terrorism by quoting Pat Buchanan from his book: <u>Where The Right Went Wrong</u>. Behind almost every act of revolutionary terror lies some political purpose. **'How other countries govern themselves is NOT a vital interest of the United States. We Americans have no commission from God to police the world'.** There cannot be an American solution to every problem. Our unquestioned support for Israel is universally resented and costing us dearly. When Bush appeared in Bagdad, he united Islam against America. U.S. dominance of the Middle East. Is not the corrective of terror. It is the cause of terror. Were we not over there, the nine eleven terrorist would not have been over here. '**Terrorism is the price of empire. If we do not wish to pay the price, we must give up the empire'.**

Expect: to have to provide for yourself so buy your own food stuff now.

Moreover Bush's "War on terrorism" was designed politically to so deprive the American people of their basic human and democratic right to the good life as to get them to foolishly accept Bush's dumb worldview, idiotic ideology and stupid foreign policy instead of getting their own needs met. Whereas **the Bible does not say that democracy is God's gift to man or that it is God's will for America to spread democracy to bring about world peace, especially Mideast peace.** In fact, the Bible does say, and Bush and now Obama had better heed this: **"If any will not provide for his own, especially those of his own house he has denied the faith and is worse than an infidel" (I Timothy 5:8).**

The Bible also says in the twenty fourth psalm that "the earth is the Lord's", so why don't we stop trying to control it and let God have it back to do with as He will!

Besides all this physical abuse during the Civil War, there were many atrocities. Just like in domestic violence there is not only the assault of a loved one, but also the pschycological and mental torture of the victim. Lincoln not only waged a war of physical conflict and an invasion upon the South, but also a mental conflict between two opinions as to the type of federal government the constitution really envisioned for the American people.

Lincoln's "reeducation house" was Fort Lafayette in New York harbor known as the "American Bastille". It was a filthy old fort crowded with the stinking bodies of the many political prisoners of the Lincoln Administration. Its beds consisted of mattresses made of straw or moss and infested with body lice, fleas, cockroaches and other vermin. The food there was horrible, too. Some occupants recorded that their breakfast consisted of "some discolored beverage, dignified by the name of coffee, a piece of fried pork, sometimes raw and sometimes half cooked, and coarse bread cut in large thick slices." Some days the water that was served at meals "would contain a dozen tadpoles from a quarter to half an inch long". Of course the guards were "insolent", and the warden or commandant, since it was a military prison "took no apparent interest in the comfort of prisoners." Among these political prisoners were newspaper editors from around the country who dared to question Lincoln's invasion of the South.

You remember from American history; Seward of Seward's Folly fame, who at that time headed Lincoln's secret police which scoured the countryside to apprehend any editors of newspapers that did not support Lincoln's war policies to arrest and imprison them there.

This policy of Lincoln's suppression of the press began with the New York City newspapers including the <u>New York Daily News</u> and <u>The Journal of Commerce</u>. These two newspapers had to be shut down for they were the leaders of the opposition press and contained many articles opposed to Lincoln's war policy, which were then reprinted in many other papers.

For these newspaper articles to get reprinted by other local newspapers they had to first reach those other newspapers. This was just usually done by the U. S. mail. But in May of 1861, <u>The Journal of Commerce</u> published a list of over one hundred northern newspapers that had editorialized against going to war and adopting Lincoln's war policy. The infuriated Lincoln Administration promptly ordered their Postmaster General to deny these papers use of the U.S. mail. Since at that time all U.S. newspaper circulation was done by mail, this illegal order put these opposition newspapers out of business. **So much for 'freedom of the press'! Yes, many of Lincoln's war policies like this one were clearly unconstitutional.**

Expect: The unconstitutional.

Among those newspapers so censored by Lincoln were the two New York newspapers already mentioned. Plus <u>The Daybook</u>, <u>Brooklyn Eagle</u>, and <u>Freeman's Journal</u> also of New York. Along with <u>The Chicago Times</u>, <u>The Dayton Empire,</u> <u>Louisville Courier</u>, <u>The Maryland</u> <u>News Sheet</u>, <u>Baltimore Gazette</u>, <u>Daily Loyalist,</u> <u>Wheeling Register</u>, and <u>Louisville True Presbyterian,</u> Among other smaller newspapers too numerous to mention.

Dean Sprague in his book, <u>Freedom under Lincoln</u> has brought out that this policy whereby Lincoln actually suppressed the news and twisted it to fit his liking had the long term impact of "laying the groundwork for such centralized coercive governmental power measures as military conscription and the federal income tax." He goes on to say; "at the outbreak of the war the federal government was not a real source of power. But when the arm of the Lincoln Administration reached into Cooperstown, New York and took away George Browne, when it slipped into Freedom, Maine and spirited away Robert Elliot, when it proved powerful enough to send three citizens of North Branch, Michigan to Fort Lafayette, and imprison, without any recourse of law, a man in Newborn, Iowa it was apparent that the federal executive had real power and that 'father Abraham' had been born to the American people."

As the fatalities from the Civil War multiplied, The Peace Movement in the North grew stronger and more vocal, and its repression by the Lincoln Administration became more severe. The editor of <u>The Essex County Democrat</u> of Haverhill, Massachusetts, was tarred and feathered by a mob of Unionists who also destroyed the papers printing equipment. Gradually the same thing happened to <u>The Sentinel</u> of Easton, Pennsylvania, <u>The Jeffersonian</u> of West Chester, Pennsylvania; <u>The Democrat</u> of Stark County Ohio; <u>The Farmer</u> of Fairfield, Connecticut and other newspapers too. All of these newspapers were known as 'peace advocates' for they editorialized in favor of ending all the bloodshed of the Civil War in working out some kind of a peaceful solution which included compensated emancipation, that many nations of that time had already done peacefully. Lincoln would have none of it, so he sent both his military and his supporters to destroy newspaper after newspaper in the North to silence The Peace Movement there. Thus The Northern Peace Movement was not only intimidated, but also physically assaulted and destroyed. Thus Fort Lafayette was filled with newspaper editors from all over the country who had dared to question the wisdom of Lincoln's military invasion of the South and his war of conquest against it. But newspaper editors were not the only political prisoners in Fort Lafayette.

A Maryland college professor; Thomas J. Delorenzo says in his book about: The Real Lincoln that "in May 1861 a special election was held to fill the ten empty seats of the Maryland House of Delegates". The men elected to fill those positions were all high-class important people, composed of leading industrialists, physicians, and judges, including lawyers from Baltimore. But because they were suspected of harboring secessionist sympathies by the Lincoln Administration, most of them were arrested without charge and sent to Fort Lafayette without trial. Some of them managed somehow to flee but Dean Sprague explains, "This was perhaps the only election in American History in which every man who was nominated and elected went to prison." Too bad corrupt politicians today go free while the innocent are sent to prison too.

By September of that same year the entire state of Maryland was under military occupation. Lincoln in Washington was taking no chances that Confederates could surround him. So he would not let the Maryland Legislature convene to discuss or vote on whether or not Maryland was to remain neutral or join the Confederacy. Therefore he sought to prohibit it from doing so by military force. One of his generals threatened to bombard Annapolis if the legislature met there, so they met in Frederic, Maryland instead. Lincoln gave another one of his generals the order to allow the Unionist members of the legislature to meet but not The Peace Party members. Lincoln's Secretary of War told his generals; "If necessary, all or any part of the members of the Maryland Legislature must be arrested." All of the members of the legislature from the Baltimore area were subsequently arrested, without any due process and including the mayor of Baltimore plus their U.S. Congressman, Henry May. All other Maryland Legislatures who were even suspected of having any secessionist sympathies were arrested too. Along with these victims of false arrest were several newspaper editors and owners from Baltimore. All these people after being arrested without cause were imprisoned without trial in Fort Lafayette. **(You might say that Fort Lafayette was the Guantanamo Bay prison of its day for Americans with constitutional rights).** From Republican Presidents Lincoln to Bush, history does repeat itself. Now doesn't it?

At the time when the Maryland Legislature went to Frederick, the entire town was sealed off by the military, under Lincoln's orders, and a house-to-house search was conducted for any Maryland Legislatures who were not friendly to the Lincoln Administration. The general in charge of this abuse, General Banks reported to Lincoln that every single advocate for peace in the Maryland Legislature had been both arrested and imprisoned.

That November other elections were scheduled to occur. These were suppressed in democratic America, the land of the free. General Banks was ordered to send troops to the voting places to protect Union voters so that their votes would count but to arrest and hold in confinement till after the election all Disunionists or peace advocates of the Peace Party. **Was this not officially sanctioned voter fraud somewhat like Bush's 'legitimate' Florida vote?**

Election judges there were instructed to forbid anyone voting against Lincoln's war. The ballots were made of different colors so that the soldiers could easily throw out any Peace Party vote and then arrest the voter. "Many who attempted to vote the Peace ticket in Baltimore Maryland were arrested for carrying a ballot of the wrong color. They were charged for 'polluting the ballot box.'" Thus Lincoln's Republican candidates won every single election in Maryland. Sprague writes; **"The orgy of the suppression of civil liberties reached its apex in Maryland"**. "Under the protection of 'Federal Bayonets', similar suppression of free elections occurred in most other northern states." **Yes, America has a history of voter fraud long before the Presidential election of 2000 in Florida!**

Expect: Your elections to get stolen too.

Time has not healed this process of fraud, for in their book; Vote Scam: The Stealing of America two brothers who are investigative journalists from the Miami area, Jim and Ken Collier, document how that **for nearly twenty years former state attorney and attorney general, Janet Reno, of Waco Massacre fame, covered up the ramped voter cheating and outright fraud common in local Florida elections. That is, the voting machines of the butterfly ballot with chads were rigged in hundreds of precincts so that only pre-approved candidates could win.** Thus with help of unscrupulous Cuban immigrants who had achieved political power in South Florida Bush was enabled to easily steal the Florida vote of the 2000 presidential elections. **Apparently from Lincoln to Bush the Republicans are still up to stealing elections. But the Democrats also do this too.**

Republican President Abraham Lincoln suspended Habeas Corpus as part of his presidential war powers on April 27, 1861. Habeas Corpus was a right or weapon for the defense of the common man first signed into English common law by King John in about A.D. 1215 via the Magna Carter. This rule of English common law set down the legal procedure for a prisoner of the state to be released from prison. Among those rights now guaranteed jailed American citizens are: the constitutional right to a speedy public trial by an impartial jury of one's peers, to be informed of the nature and cause of the accusation against them, to be confronted with witnesses against them, to bring witnesses in their favor, and to have the assistance of legal counsel. Republican President Abraham Lincoln, or I should say; 'Lincoln the Magnificent', **Sovereign** of the U. S.A. suspended all these constitutional rights in 1861 and his suspension of them remained in effect for Lincoln's entire Administration, even after the Civil War ended. Does not this same condition exist with another former Republican President George W. Bush?

Upon taking office in March 1861, Lincoln the deceitful also implemented a whole series of unconstitutional acts, including the invasion of the South without even consulting Congress, blockading southern ports, and declaring Martial Law. Afterward, he suspended Habeas Corpus.

With that suspension of Habeas Corpus together with his Martial Law decree thousands of American citizens were imprisoned without trial after being arrested without charge.

Expect: Marshal Law and imprisonment without trial.

'Lincoln the Magnificent' Martial Law decree in the North enabled his military to arrest and imprison thousands of American citizens, sometimes on just mere rumors, which led to the false imprisonment of thousands of antiwar protestors in Fort Lafayette. By 1862, 'Lincoln the Magnificent' suspension of Habeas Corpus had been expanded to include those who 'discouraged voluntary enlistments' in Lincoln's war. His Martial Law enabled the military to bypass all civil liberty protections to arrest and imprison many thousands of citizens too. So American citizens of the North were subjected to this unconstitutional abuse for the duration of the Lincoln Administration. Prisoners were never told why, or for what reason they were being arrested, no investigations of any kind were ever made, and no trials were ever held. Doesn't this sound like the forerunner of George W. Bush's and Barack Obama's Guantanamo Bay for Americans?

'Lincoln the Magnificent' also censored all telegraphic communication, nationalized railroads, created several new states, ordered his troops to interfere with free elections in the North by intimidating Democratic voters there and deporting Congressman Clement L. Vallasdingham of Ohio, **and confiscated private property including firearms in violation of the Second Amendment.**

Expect: The confiscation of private property including firearms in violation of the Second Amendment.

This unconstitutional abuse of the civil liberties of American citizens went as far as the passage of the Indemnity Act of 1863, which placed President Lincoln his cabinet and his military above the law. **Today's Patriot Act of similar design also squashes the civil liberties of American citizens just like Lincoln's Indemnity Act of 1863 did. Obviously times have not really changed that much, although President Obama promised real change. What was first instituted by President Lincoln and reintroduced by President Bush has now been reinforced by President Obama and made into official public policy. So watch out and get prepared NOW as War is certainly coming. The Lord Jesus said so!**

Review of What to Expect from the American Civil War

Page 153. In any war usually those who win the war write the history of it that is approved to be taught in school. But here through God's prophetic gifting we get to say some truthful things that need to be said.

Page 154. This same problem also exists today. America has been warned repeatedly to get out of Japan, Germany, Korea and now many Muslim lands but refuses to do so. Such invites tragedy and causes outlandish expense being passed on to our children in the form of deficit spending.

EXPECT: More deficit spending even (war on credit).

Page 154. At the beginning of the Civil War many commissioned officers felt that this was just a dispute and not worthy of total war. President Lincoln went through many gentleman generals until he found a few savage rouges (drunks) in uniform that would do Lincoln's bidding.

Page 155. The Bible says that there is nothing new under the sun (Ecclesiastes 1:9). Sure that many real patriots resent the Patriot ACT and the loss of liberty imposed recently on us by George Bush 43. Actually Lincoln had a similar modus operandi plus Lincoln also had people held without trial and in some cases without charge. The conditions of the prisons that Lincoln used would also be considered a war crime today.

Page 156. As you know the Bible has been taken out of school, but it still says in Numbers 32:23 'Be sure your sin will find you out'. And the Lord Jesus said in Luke 12:2 'for there is nothing covered that shall not be revealed, neither hid that shall not be known'.

Your Bible is your Guidebook to keep you free from sin. Study it!

Page 159. Entitlements begin with Sovereignty and with the Republican President Abraham Lincoln, 'The Magnificent'.

EXPECT: Someone else's entitlement to cause you to do without, so get your stuff NOW!

Page 159. Lincoln thanked Sheridan's Army for doing this in this way since he believed that 'might makes right' and he could ignore the Constitution, the Geneva Convention and common decency and morality as long as his military won. If Lincoln lost, he knew that he and his top generals would be hung as war criminals, because that's just what they were!

EXPECT: The War Crimes of Total War. And any War to be a Total War.

Page 160. Many slaves who ended up in the hands of the Union army were not set free despite the Emancipation Proclamation, but were put to work doing the most unpleasant work in and around army encampments. In short, **Lincoln's Emancipation Proclamation was only applied to rebel territory.**

Page 160. Lincoln maintained that his Emancipation Proclamation was just 'a war power' that he had the power to declare since the U.S. was at war. In reality, the President had no such power at that time to dictate such to any state. Today of course presidents routinely dictate thousands of laws, regulations and executive orders that they also fail to fund to every state and local government. It was the Republican President Abraham Lincoln who started this.

EXPECT: Unfunded executive orders that will cost you dearly.

Page 160. Hostile white immigrant mobs had assaulted Blacks in northern cities for years, so in July 1863 there

were <u>race riots in New York City</u> as Whites protested both the Emancipation Proclamation and Lincoln's new conscription law.

<u>EXPECT: race riots so be sure you live in an area that is at least 90% your own race to avoid racial conflict, or to be safe move to a safe place that is.</u>

Page 161. At this time the <u>mayhem in New York City</u> was atrocious. The streetlights were out, many hangings and murders occurred as terror and anxiety was common. All the shops were closed and business was at a standstill. All carriages and buses had ceased running. Telegraph wires were cut, and even railroad tracks were torn up. No Black person dared to show themselves on that day. Colored people weren't even safe in their own homes.

<u>EXPECT: mayhem, so move to a safe place now.</u>

Page 161. The very idea that the Civil War happened because the people in the North adopted abolitionist feelings and were morally constrained to free the slaves is obviously fraudulent. For no abolitionist was ever elected to any major political office in any Northern state. The overwhelming majority of White Northerners cared little if at all about the welfare of slaves and treated Blacks that lived among them with contempt, ridicule, discrimination, and even violence.

Page 162. The Author Eugene Berwanger describes the condition of Blacks in the North at this time in his book: <u>North of Slavery</u> that: **"In virtually every phase of existence (In the North), Negroes found themselves systematically separated from Whites. They were either excluded from railway cars, omnibuses stage coaches, and steam boats or assigned to special 'Jim Crow' sections; they sat, when permitted, in secluded and removed corners of theaters and lecture halls; they could not enter most hotels, restaurants, and resorts, except as servants: they prayed**

in 'Negro pews' in the White churches, and if partaking of the Sacrament of the Lord's Supper, they waited until the Whites had been served the bread and wine. Moreover, they were often educated in segregated schools, punished in segregated prisons, nursed in segregated hospitals and buried in segregated cemeteries".

Page 163. Lincoln believed that he should have the consolidation of all state power in him, the elected <u>Sovereign.</u>

Page 163. Additionally, history records that the Federal Soldiers routinely robbed everyone at gunpoint and in broad daylight during the mayhem of the Civil War.

<u>**EXPECT; Robbery by government officials and troops not just gangs.**</u>

Page 163. Mark Grimsley records in his book: <u>The Hard Hand of War: Union Military Policy</u> toward Southern Civilians, 1861-1865 **'with the utter disregard for Blacks that was the norm among Union Troops, that the soldiers ramshackled the slave cabins, taking whatever they liked'. Many accounts also record that Black woman (who were often gang raped by Union troops) suffered the most and that many Black men as a result hated the Union Armies. (The University of South Carolina has diaries, which record many rapes of Black woman right out in the public in broad daylight as if they had been caught like farm animals in heat ready to be exploited).**

<u>**EXPECT: Rape by government officials.**</u>

Page 163. Emancipation was a farce, which the Blacks could see through. For they lost not only their jobs with whatever benefits they may have earned but also their homes. In those days, a slave usually got good health care along with free housing as owners 'property care'. Once Lincoln forced his will upon the South, the Blacks were free from any job, any place to stay or any care

except Government care. <u>**This is where unemployment and government handouts like welfare came from.**</u>

<u>EXPECT: Unemployment.</u>

It was here that General Jackson earned his nickname by furiously turning back and defeating decisively an overpowering Union Force. After the battle, he approached the Confederate President, Jefferson Davis, whom he saw on the battlefield and said to him; "give me ten thousand men and I will take Washington tomorrow". Davis being the gentleman, refused. He later said that he regretted that decision for the rest of his life and considered it to be **'one of the greatest mistakes of the war'**.

Page 164. The Geneva Convention of 1863 said that any naval blockade is an act of war upon a country's civilian population as well as its armed forces. The nations of the civilized world also agreed then that it was a war crime, punishable by either death or imprisonment for armies to: (1) Attack defenseless cities and towns, (2) Plunder and destroy civilian property, (3) Take from the civilian population more than what is necessary to feed any occupying army. They also had concluded that the only just war was a defensive war. On this count alone Lincoln's invasion of the South made him a war criminal, not a hero worthy of a memorial in his honor. Moreover occupying soldiers who destroy private property, farms and houses are to be called 'Savage Barbarians 'not national heroes.

<u>Expect: Unconventional, uncivilized, barbaric, non-Geneva Conventional War.</u>

Page 168. They did not steel out of any need, but simply stole out of greed and pure meanness.

Page 169. To get rid of these 'low life scavengers', when ever Sherman's army came to a river or stream that they had to cross, first after his army built a bridge of pontoons

they would cross over them then they dismantled the pontoons and removed them before the Blacks had a chance to follow. (Since Blacks could not swim and feared the water they had to stay in the South and starve and could not migrate north).

Page 172. As I have shown and as the historical facts confirm both generals Sheridan and Sherman were in effect terrorists of their day for they not only burnt civilians alive, both also slaughtered farm animals burnt barns and crops and looted and torched cities. They made their destructive abuses and war crimes against humanity into legitimate acts of war.

<u>**Expect: War Crimes to become legitimate acts of war.**</u>

Page 173. While we condemn terror, it succeeds and will be employed again and again to achieve goals worth dying for.

<u>**Expect: Terrorism**</u>

Page 174. 'One man's terrorist is another man's freedom fighter'.

Page 174. We Americans have no commission from God to police the world.

Page 175. **The Bible does not say that democracy is God's gift to man or that it is God's will for America to spread democracy to bring about world peace, especially Mideast peace.** In fact, the Bible does say, and Bush had better heed this: **"If any will not provide for his own, especially those of his own house he has denied the faith and is worse than an infidel"(I Timothy 5:8).**

"Terrorism is the price of empire, if we do not wish to pay the price we must give up the empire"

<u>**Expect: To have to provide for yourself, so buy your own food now!**</u>

Page 175. The Bible also says in the twenty fourth psalm that "**the earth is the Lord's",** so why don't we stop trying to control it and let God have it back to do with as He will!

Page 176. So much for 'freedom of the press'! Yes, many of Lincoln's war policies like this one were clearly unconstitutional.

<u>**Expect: The unconstitutional.**</u>

Page 179. That November other elections were scheduled to occur. These were suppressed in democratic America, the land of the free.

Page 180. "The orgy of the suppression of civil liberties reached its apex in Maryland". "Under the protection of 'Federal Bayonets', similar suppression of free elections occurred in most other northern states." **Yes, America has a history of voter fraud long before the Presidential election of 2000 in Florida!**

Page 180. For nearly twenty years former state attorney and attorney general, Janet Reno, of Waco Massacre fame, covered up the ramped voter cheating and outright fraud common in local Florida elections. That is, the voting machines of the butterfly ballot with chads were rigged in hundreds of precincts so that only pre-approved candidates could win.

Page 180. Apparently from Lincoln to Bush the Republicans are still up to stealing elections and illegal immigration shows that the Democrats do this too.

<u>**Expect: Your elections to get stolen too.**</u>

Page 180. Republican President Abraham Lincoln suspended Habeas Corpus as part of his presidential war powers on April 27, 1861.

<u>**Expect: Habeas Corpus to get suspended for you too.**</u>

Page 181. Upon taking office in March 1861, Lincoln the deceitful also implemented a whole series of unconstitutional acts, including the invasion of the South without even consulting Congress, blockading Southern ports, and declaring Martial Law. Afterward, he suspended Habeas Corpus.

Page 181. With that suspension of Habeas Corpus together with his Martial Law decree thousands of American citizens were imprisoned in Fort Lafayette without trial after being arrested without charge.

Expect: Marshall Law and imprisonment without trail.

Page 182. And confiscated private property including firearms in violation of the Second Amendment.

Expect: The confiscation of private property including your firearms in violation of the second amendment.

Page 182. This unconstitutional abuse of the Civil Liberties of American citizens went as far as the passage of the Indemnity Act of 1863, which placed President Lincoln and his cabinet and his military above the law. **Today's Patriot Act of similar design also squashes the civil liberties of American citizens just like Lincoln's Indemnity Act of 1863 did. Obviously times have not really changed that much, although President Obama promised real change. What was first instituted by President Lincoln and reintroduced by President Bush has now been reinforced by President Obama and made into official public policy. So watch out and get prepared NOW!**

Famines

In the same verse **(Matthew 24:7)**, the Lord Jesus also states that famines will come. The dictionary calls a famine a drastic and wide-spread shortage of food. This shortage of food is most often caused naturally by drought (a failure to rain sufficient enough for crops to grow). Those of you living in the Midwest (America's bread basket) know full well that there has been insufficient rain to enable crops to grow but now there are floods.

This nationwide drought has also reduced the water level required to float barges loaded with grain down the Mississippi River and load them onto ships for export. This means that unless rainfall happens soon that river will not be able to sustain barge traffic. So even if by some miracle grain does grow in the heartland it will still not be able to reach the Port of New Orleans to be shipped to starving countries.

Much of the free world depends on America's grain. So famine here has worldwide implications and is very unpleasant indeed. Famine can also result in mob violence, social upheaval, rebellion, terrorism and even war on the world stage. And assault, robbery and an atmosphere of crime locally caused by being forced to do without, being unnecessarily deprived and somehow cheated out of the basics of life.

The Apostle Jim Bakker of the www.Jimbakkershow.com has already seen famine coming in a vision from God. I therefore recommend that you either contact his website listed above or call his phone number at 1-888-988-1588 in order to get a catalog to procure his products to ensure your survival.

Famine has other causes one of which concerns the political status of nations and weather they are at war. First let's consider political status. The author of a book called <u>Democracy as Freedom</u> affirms political propaganda by saying that 'no famine has ever taken place in the history of the world in a functioning democracy'. If this statement is true, then what about the potato famine in Ireland, a region of supposedly democratic Great Britain?

The British apparently tried to do to the Irish what the Americans had done to their American Indian Tribes (exterminate them). Only the American government did so by donating small pox contaminated blankets to their Indians while the British slaughtered 5/6 of the Irish population by 1650. Then the British followed this up with their Penal Laws.

These Penal Laws specifically prevented the creation of any government relief programs for the Irish to feed their unemployed and themselves. This was because many thought that spending English money on feeding the dying Irish was a poor investment as the welfare of Irish peasants just didn't make any sense to the English aristocracy who regarded the Irish as a beggarly and sickly race of misfits not worth saving.

Excuse me; I guess this revelation is not seen as being politically correct. However this truth does not come from me alone but is also documented on pages 115 and 123 in the book called: The Fourth Horseman. To further reinforce this truth it must also be said that the constant occupation of Ireland lead to the closing down of Ireland's famous woolen industry whereby 30,000 people were put out of factory work and now work in the fields of the potatoe patch thus the British stole Ireland's woolen industry.

So by 1851 famine had buried 2 million Irish and had sent another 2 million overseas. Therefore today there are fewer people living in Ireland now than lived there in 1800.

Actually Ireland was doing fairly well after the Middle Ages. Back then the common people were eating meat from their own herds. But after hundreds of years of abuse by the English, their normal diet gradually disintegrated. It went from meat to oats and then from oats to potatoes.

The first potatoes reached Ireland from Spain about 1580. Potatoes are a New World vegetable that the Spanish introduced.

Potatos provided the peasants of Ireland with more than twice the protein now recommended daily for the average adult. They also provide three times the vitamin C and 3 times the Iron needed each day. Plus since they grow underground, they could also be hidden from the British.

The potato was also very valuable because it protected the Irish people from scurvy and other vitamin deficiency diseases. I also eat potatoes for they supply potassium which reduces my high blood pressure.

So the potato sustained Irish life, but maybe it's not wise 'to have all your your eggs in one basket'. In other words it would have been better to have a balanced diet but poverty resulting from occupation prohibited that. When the potato blight struck in 1845 about 9 million Irish peasants were consuming potatoes. But these 9 million were not 'well fed'.

Other than war and occupation which I will discuss, the Irish potatoe blight was partly caused naturally by the fungus: 'Phytopthora infestans' which sent millions of the Irish to either Old World graves or New World ghettos. This fungus was a natural companion to the potatoe. However it was usually dormant. In 1845 the weather of Ireland suddenly changed. That year it grew much colder and frosted that spring to abuse the young potatoe plants. On top of all this it rained continuously for several weeks and drowned out the fields where the potatoes were. Thus the potatoes rotted and stunk.

While we're discussing this potatoe famine we should remember that the potatoe is very beneficial especially for subsistence farming. **No other agricultural crop, grown on just 1 acre of land can feed a grown man, his wife and up to 6 children the way potatoes can. Plus they naturally hide from rampaging armies.**

But among natural calamities drought, not excessive rain stricts and destroys more crops. In Latin America for example those unlucky people who can no longer feed themselves or their families simply have no choice but to look north to enter the United States illegally in their search of food stamps, since there is no available work. Others so afflicted must leave their rural communities for urban slums searching often fruitlessly for any means of support in their own poor countries that are also suffering.

The natural calamity cause for famine also includes floods, storms with excessive rain or hail at the wrong time in the growing season, tornadoes, hurricanes and earthquakes with tsunamis.

Of course war is a major factor that causes famines. In fact The New Republic magazine says in its article about the end of hunger that famine has taken many more lives through recorded history than war. So as we have seen war is not the only cause of famine but it still is a major cause of famine.

If war were to strike the American homeland we already know what to expect. To refresh your memory let me state again: **Page 172: As I have shown and as the historical facts confirm both generals Sheridan and Sherman were in effect terrorists of their day for they not only burnt civilians alive, both also slaughtered farm animals alive, burnt barns and crops and looted and torched cities. They made their destructive abuses and war crimes against humanity into legitimate acts of war.**

To better update this lets consider the Afghanistan War in the National Catholic Reporter of November 22, 2002 on page 13 that article reveals that the efforts to provide humanitarian relief was undermined by American alliances with various war lords. So this complication prolongs the famine and deepens its consequences.

In the modern era, it is commonly believed that famine has been outgrown by society's advances especially in technology. But advances in technology do not ensure agricultural advances, especially with genetically modified foods.

Author William Emgdahl of the book: '**Seeds of Destruction'** said over coasttocoastam.com radio on May 2, 2013, that France found that rats fed a diet of Monsanto genetically modified corn over 2 years had an alarming incidence of cancer tumors, organ damage and early deaths. This is supposedly one of the ways that healthier foods are supposed to reduce the earth's population. Other more visible methods include wars, disease and vaccines. Almost no one would consider engineered foods that are supposedly healthier to be an agent of death. But that skillfully researched book shows just how a small socio-political American elite seeks to establish its control over the very basis of human survival: the provision of our daily bread. **'Control the food and you control the people'. Obviously this is a totalitarian mindset which also results in famine just like any authoritarian world view and this control comes through genetically modified seeds that no one would suspect. (The Anti-Christ will master such deception as the 'mark of the beast' that no one will be able to buy or sell without).**

The magazine: 'The Ecologist' of September 2000 reveals on page 26 that having sewed the seed of famine in Ethiopia through such structural adjustment as the IMF and the world bank through free trade by enabling U.S. multinationals to exploit the disaster by providing genetically modified seeds as aid. This economic therapy (imposed austerity) under the IMF and the World Bank's jurisdiction is in large part responsible for triggering famine and social devastation in Ethiopia and the rest of sub-Saharan Africa, wrecking the peasant economy and impoverishing millions of people.

Not long ago the White House tapes of former President John F. Kennedy revealed that as an independently wealthy man he was against the Federal Reserve's strangle hold on the American economy and wanted to abolish it. But he got shot to death in Dallas, TX on November 22, 1963. So the Federal Reserve survived to screw all Americans under Obama. So when the famine comes you now know who to blame. Instead of wasting billions on Wall Street the Federal Reserve could have given every American $56,000.00. Just think with that much money you could have bought a farm or even gone into some organic business.

This will not be politically correct but it must be said: Famine also results from spiritual judgment on the sin of worshipping false gods like Allah on your land. And drought a basic cause of famine also results from allowing the followers of false gods like Allah to pollute the land with their presence. **So be sure that there are no Muslims around where you live and better yet move to that place that has the highest percentage of fundamental Christians per capita for your own good.**

So famines will happen again and again. Even our best intentions of extinguishing them actually invite them as I have now shown. Dearly beloved **expect famines, because the Lord Jesus said that they will come.**

Pestilences

After the Apostle Jim Bakker first shared his unpleasant vision about 31 bad things coming in the last days, an old unnamed prophet shared with him about the next unpleasant problem coming our way according to the Lord Jesus is pestilences. The dictionary says that pestilences are usually fatal epidemic diseases that can be carried and infect you by contaminating agents, usually insects. I am sure that many of you have heard about The West Nile Virus. This disease is being presented on the public airways as a naturally occurring disease.

Actually West Nile Virus was a biological weapon Saddam Hussein bought from America back in the 1980's. When American troops entered Iraq in the Iraq War they blew up these bombs. Of course some of that virus contamination got on their clothes. And even though their clothes were washed many times over there still small mosquito eggs contaminated with West Nile Virus came home with the troops.

The proof of this is the fact that West Nile Virus is mainly found in Texas where most of our troops are also from and where they went home to.

This unfortunate problem arose primarily because the so called Christian, George Bush 43 failed to have on his staff any Biblical advisor that knew from the scriptures that the Euphrates river of Iraq contains four fallen angels with the prescribed authority to kill 1/3 of mankind in these last days (Revelations 9:14 & 15). Knowing this George Bush or any reasonable man would have avoided this Iraq war. Yes the weapons of mass destruction were really there in this form and are just now coming home to bite us.

This West Nile Virus is only one pestilence. But notice that the word; pestilences is plural, so others will come that we don't know about yet. We can get ready to protect ourselves by getting the Silver Sol Starter Kit for $110.00 by calling 1-888-988-1588 (this kit also contains lozenges and combats respiratory infections like bird flu, swine flu and even the common cold). It is also a great disinfectant and an unusual healing crème for very bad burns. It also kills even superbug viruses like EBOLA and AIDS that are resistant to other medicines.

Another one of these pestilences is Obama's EBOLA. Although this disease comes from Africa, Obama America's first part Black president has initiated policies to make the American people own this disease as if it were really theirs.

The Obama Administration has not told the American people the whole truth about this disease. For one, while they criticized former president Bush for sending the National Guard to fight in Iraq. Obama is also sending the National Guard to fight EBOLA in West Africa as if this disease, a dangerous mutating virus could be killed by armed forces. Moreover, EBOLA is not just an upper resperatory disease that kills by bleeding to death but also a sexually transmitted disease.

If a Black man miraculously recovers from EBOLA, he wants to celebrate his victory over this cursed disease and prove that he's still alive by having sex. This is how the main problem arises. For the EBOLA virus is still transmitted right along with his semen for two months after recovery. Thus their sex partners catch EBOLA too.

The Black Liberian man who came to America in order to have sex with his girlfriend here and lied in order to do so. While lying is just a minor sin, it appears that lying now about this results in death since 'the wages of sin is death'.

This points out another major hazard that comes with EBOLA. That is Black people are particularly susceptible to this disease. For the sake of the welfare of our own African American (Black) population those exposed to EBOLA in the countries where they live should be forbidden to enter our country.

I don't suppose that this position will be adopted until one of the two nurses who caught EBOLA in Texas dies. The Asian nurse may recover. But the Afro American nurse as a Black women may not. If this happens the Black population of America for their own welfare will insist that the Obama Administration keep those infected with EBOLA out of this country.

Among these catastrophic pestilences is one that happened here in America not too long ago. Actually this epidemic was so wide spread that it was a pandemic. Pandemics usually last for up to a year or more, so you must prepare for them by getting a year's supply of food, a silver kit as I recommended, also getting a good quality first aid kit and if a health emergency is declared move away from people. Consider your health and your life more important than maintaining your social base of friends and relatives. Yes your life is more important than even your job or getting a good education. What good is a good education or even a first rate marriage proposal if you wind up dead?

The pandemic I need to discuss here was the one involving smallpox. Before it was supposedly eradicated by vaccination it killed many people. Today for supposedly research purposes a small sample of smallpox is being kept by both the United States and Russia. It appears to me that this small sample of smallpox is being held in reserve as a possible future biological weapon.

Let me share how smallpox was used as a biological weapon here in America in the past. But before I impart this shocking news please sit down and if you have a heart condition or high blood pressure or a nervous stomach or depression you might need to take a pill first. You Christians should have already taken the Gospel (Gos-pill). Whereby you already know that 'the servant is not greater than his Lord' and whatever He suffered will eventually come your way too (John 15:20).

If you are now comfortable, you're ready to hear what the school books hid: I can now tell you that smallpox arrived in the New World shortly after Columbus landed. It was brought deliberately as a biological weapon by an infected Negro slave carrier to eradicate the AmerIndians of the West Indies who would not work the sugar plantations there. So West African slaves were brought in by the Spanish to do the work instead. In fact before 1800 there were more Black slaves in the Americas than White Americans. (This is where slavery first happened in America and not in the Confederate South).

Because smallpox seemed to quickly eradicate the AmerIndians while sparing the Spanish it led to the eventual medical adoption of vaccination. Some medical experts back in those days realized the Spanish were spared because many of them had already encountered smallpox as children in Spain. Were now pox marked and immune to further smallpox infections for the rest of their lives.

Therefore Cortez took with him the immune Spanish and an infected Negro slave carrier of smallpox to do genocide on the Aztec Indians, to strip them of their land and there gold. They infected with smallpox Montezuma the Aztec king and killed him. And reduced the Aztec population from about 25 million to just over 6 million within 10 years. (For you Blacks that are upset over this, no its not racism but just historical fact).

Black slaves were once used back then as carriers of Smallpox. Today some Blacks carry Aids. Thanks to the integration of schools, your public school has now become the ideal breeding ground for Aids as 10% of all Black males carry AIDS. And thanks to the civil rights of interracial relationships this disease (Aids) is now a wholesale infector of all communities. **What good are civil rights that kill you?**

The smallpox epidemic was considered the shock troops of the Spanish conquest. It was used successfully to depopulate the Americas of Indians. To take both their land for settlements and colonies and their gold to fund a new crusade against the Muslims who were the enemies of Catholic Spain and had just conquered Byzantine (the eastern Roman Empire). (Historically this is what the gold was to be used for).

The Spanish had to fight against the Muslim Mores in order to liberate Spain their homeland. One of the places that they recovered is called Granada. The Muslims in New York City wanted to name their new mosque by ground zero that same name (Granada) in order to show that they had taken it back as a prize of Muslim conquest.

While I'm discussing this Muslim curse I need to state emphatically that Allah is a false god. And the mistaken tolerance of former president George W. Bush by saying that Muslim is a religion of peace is also false. Muslim **(Moslem or Islam) is not a religion of peace but a totalitarian ideology of conquest as the name of their new mosque in New York City confirms).**

For those who think that I'm just being a Bush basher let me bring out this truth about former Democratic President and still infidel Bill Clinton who despised and rejected the Christian history of Serbia in stopping the Muslim invasion of Europe and ordered our troops to bomb Christian Serbs to ensure a Muslim foothold in Europe called Bosnia. Now Obama the nominal Muslim is opening up America to Muslim Attack and got his Obama care in place to care for the collateral damage of the innocent casualties.

This biological warfare was called by some 'The Hand of God working on the side of the right' and by others 'the live coal that burned its way clear through Mexico'. Some even rejoiced and said that the Spanish with the smallpox infected Negro slave carrier of smallpox 'bravely worked the smallpox for Cortez and the superior civilization'.

When America (the United States) was founded this same policy of colonization through genocide was adopted and then employed by the US Government when it donated smallpox infected blankets to the Indians.

Oh my God how could you know these things? Because 'The eyes of the Lord run to and fro upon the whole earth and are in everyplace beholding the evil and the good' (Proverbs 15:3). And as a Christian I have access to all that God wants me to know.

My words here are also supported in part by Dr. R.S. Bray in his book: <u>Armies of Pestilence the Impact of Disease on History.</u>

This smallpox pandemic is mainly of the past like Yellow Fever and The Black Death Plague. Today there are other serious diseases like E. Coli, Malaria, Typhus, Cholera, Dengue Fever and various forms of Influenza. But the main ones now are both the sexually transmitted diseases AIDS and EBOLA

Some years ago as some were studying various prison systems, it was discovered that the state of Alabama gave each new convict destined to become one of their inmates an HIV blood test in order to discover who had AIDS. This was done to separate the infected inmates from the general prison population.

Today however with all these liberal politics of Civil Rights and anti-discrimination policies it's almost impossible to quarantine anyone from infecting the rest of us. So the advance of these diseases, pestilences and contaminants are almost guaranteed now by law. A liberal government makes it now certain that these afflictions will be coming your way.

For example, in your integrated public schools every student should be blood tested to see who has AIDS. As you well know, there are fights in school and we don't want to see some contaminated person bleeding on the innocent or some juvenile conman killing your daughter with AIDS disguised as love. It should be made public knowledge that at least 10% of all Black males carry AIDS. You should know the medical facts on this issue for your own protection. No, it's not racism but truth.

Another one of these diseases is Enterovirus D68 a type of reverse smallpox biological warfare where Latino Indian children from Central America get to infect predominately white American children with this polio like plague. It should be noted that the Obama Administration has imported these contaminated Indian children into every state and even paid for their air fare with your taxes. In hope that someday they'll grow up to vote liberal Democrat.

Local school boards who allow grown men disguised as children to invade and infest our local schools with this disease should be prosecuted. These so called 'children' that can't even read and write their own language have no right to expect us to teach them anything. **Throw them out of the country and 'have no fellowship with the unprofitable works of darkness'!**

Among these pestilences also include those that infect plants and crops. Here in Florida the orange crop (orange juice) is facing a fatal epidemic called 'Citrus Greening'. In the Western United States 'Valley Fever' is coming upon the scene. Its main cause is drought which kicks up the dust that spreads the fungus that causes the disease.

Back in the days of the Jesus Movement, our dirt farmer Pastor Lyle Steenis told us about his experiences in the 'Dust Bowl' when he was a child. A big black storm cloud that looked just like a rain cloud would come up from Oklahoma to them in Kansas. When his mother saw it she would ring the dinner bell and all the kids would drop whatever they were doing and hurry home. Once they came in she gave each one either a wet washcloth or a wet kitchen towel to put over their face to keep out the dust as they fell to their own place on the kitchen floor. Those who did not take such precautions caught 'Dust Pneumonia'. Today this is called 'Valley Fever'. Since it is affecting California's agricultural heartland it's going to be costing you more at the grocery store soon as California produces one quarter of the nation's food.

It should be remembered that dust also causes famine and are both the **results of judgment for sin**. Some are so laden with sin that 'they cannot see the forest for the trees'. One quick way to resolve the drought problem in California is to get rid of all the politically accepted sin there. **That is if you want it to rain, get rid of the Muslims there as worshipping a false god curses your land.**

Some of these pestilences have come along with animals as is noted in the book: <u>The Fourth Horseman</u> by the professional writer Andrew Nikiforuk. On page 8 of that book measles had come along with dogs into our everyday lives. Tuberculosis and diphtheria had come along with cows. And the Rhino virus which causes the common cold had come along with horses. Anthrax also had come along with ranching cattle.

Some of these pestilences were used as biological weapons of war. The Arabs stopped the crusades with Malaria. The Russians stopped Napoleon with typhoid and their Russian winter.

Whatever disease or medical problem comes your way have in your medicine chest a supply of Silver Sol. This product kills all diseases including yeast, viral and biologic infections. It even works to stop antibiotic resistant diseases known as 'super bugs'. You can get it by mail for $110.00 by calling 1-888-988-1588 twenty four hours a day, 7 days a week.

Earthquakes

After this the Lord Jesus mentions earthquakes which will soon disrupt your peace and safety, and perhaps even your way of life too.

As the Apostle Jim Bakker was sharing his unpleasant vision about 31 things coming our way in these last days he mentioned earthquakes and that the Japanese earthquake would come first, and that it would be a 9.0 earthquake, doing considerable damage. Then the next big earthquake will be the Southern California earthquake. In light of this clear prophecy, if I lived in the LA area or any region out there prone to earthquakes, I'd be making my plans to relocate.

You don't want to jump out of the frying pan and into the fire though, so remember that the Midwest earthquake fault is now overdue for massive movement too.

We have learned from this massive Japanese earthquake that an earthquake can result in all kinds of tragedy that the Lord Jesus does not mention. And no one would have imagined that from an earthquake thousands of acres of good farmland would have to be abandoned by human habitation for thousands of years because of radioactive contamination from that same massive earthquake destroying nuclear power plants and a tsunami resulting from that same earthquake then pushing flood waters of radioactive residue across the land to contaminate it for thousands of years. Resulting in the unemployment of thousands of farmers and causing them to abandon their farms and way of life.

In another earthquake that happened a few years earlier in a less developed country (Haiti) the earthquake there has resulted in a cholera epidemic. Cholera is primarily a waterborne disease. And nuclear contamination is too.

The Apostle Jim Bakker has a Seychelle water filtration product that one can buy which filters out 99.999% of all contaminants including radioactive ones. (The inventor of this water filtration that removes nuclear contamination is now very famous in

Japan). With this product one can convert contaminated water full of disease, filth, chemicals, drugs and radioactivity into crystal clear 99.999% pure water to drink safely. Since your body is the temple of the Holy Ghost you might need to order this product (so call: 1-888-988-1588) to be prepared for what's coming as no reasonable person can expect to consume filth and then as a result reasonably expect to do the works of God.

Before we leave this verse we must note that the last part of it, 'IN DIVERSE PLACES' expands our vulnerability. To me this means that physical earthquakes will not only follow geological faults but can happen anywhere even in your hometown.

Also almost all dictionaries define earthquakes as a noun referring to a sudden or abrupt movement of the earth along a geological fault. This definition is definitely clear concerning physical earthquakes. But I believe the Lord Jesus has also shown me to also approach earthquakes from an adjective standpoint.

That means that an 'adjective earthquake' is one that describes abrupt or sudden changes in conditions in our everyday lives in these last days. In that sense there can be earthquakes that run the whole gambit of human experience from spiritual earthquakes resulting in revival to economic earthquakes like those caused by a stock market crash. And of course all these issues are discussed in the Bible concerning the last days. So first I'll discuss a spiritual earthquake since it's the most important and will begin America's recovery from 'demonic democracy'.

Right now for all practical purposes America appears to be frozen from spirituality in bad ideology and false doctrine. Some would say that America needs to be thawed out from political restraints in order to achieve its spirituality. Among those things it needs to be thawed out from are also stupid liberal ideology like political correctness along with this diversity delusion.

A real spiritual revival like an earthquake would happen suddenly and unexpectedly just like when the prophet said during a time of famine due to siege to the people that: 'by this time tomorrow shall a measure of fine flour be sold for a shekel and two measures of Barley for a shekel in the gate of Samaria' (II Kings 7:1).

In other words the people got abundance within one day while they were under siege and were starving to death. The prophet's message there of course was spiritual. But the result became practical economics involving the people eating abundantly. So this confirms that saying of the Lord Jesus that 'He has come that we might have life and have it more abundantly' (John 10:10).

This shows what a spiritual earthquake can do. It turns night into day and darkness into light. It gets the unemployed hired and the sick healed (Obama Care cannot heal anyone, only the Lord Jesus heals). So a spiritual earthquake can move people quickly from poverty to plenty and from depression to a life worth living.

A political earthquake once happened in this nation not too long ago, some of you might even remember it. Back then former president and still reprobate Jimmy Carter had hostages everywhere, not only in Iran but also with the economy and with his own bowels that were being held hostage due to constipation from eating too many peanuts while millions were out of work. Former president Ronald Reagan beat him by an overwhelming majority.

Now America is being held hostage again from experiencing real liberty with peace and prosperity by Obama Care, the IRS, the ATF, the Border Patrol, Homeland Security, the FBI, the Justice Department, Affirmative Action, the Muslim brotherhood, Genetically Modified Foods and even the Democratic Senate. Since **'There is a time for every purpose under the sun'(Ecclesiastes 3:1).** It's high time someone asked God to raise them up to cast these reprobates out of office just like real Christians cast out demons to restore America to what its founding fathers wanted it to be. **'You receive not because**

you ask not, ask and you shall receive' (James 4:2, John 16:24).

America also needs an economic earthquake of real recovery. When Obama first took office Black unemployment was at 15%. Then it claimed to over 19% by the start of his second time. Obama was obviously more concerned about his socialist healthcare than even with the welfare of his own people. A Bible verse applies here. The one that says: **'If any care not for his own, especially those of his own house, he has denied the faith and is worse than an infidel' (I Timothy 5:8).**

Back when Obama began to run for office he promised change, real change. But in foreign policy he has gone from the dumb to the stupid. When 9/11 happened the Saudi Arabian royal family was vacationing here in Florida at Disney World. Right after 9/11 on the day when airplanes were not supposed to fly, they were flown out of the country back to Saudi Arabia. Likewise when the Boston Marathon Bombing occurred, as Glen Beck reported an unnamed co-conspirator participant in that bombing, in order to avoid his prosecution was flown back to Saudi Arabia.

Isn't this the same reprehensible foreign policy that Bush had? This shows up again in this Benghazi, Libya fiasco when UN Ambassador Susan Rice went on all five Sunday TV talk shows to lie to the American people in order to protect the Muslim Brotherhood's revolution in Libya. This Administration did not want the American people to know that the Arab Spring's supposed revolutions for democracy were really for the expansion of the Muslim Brotherhood instead.

Earthquakes usually symbolize God's judgment. Presently an earthquake of some sort will suddenly come as God's judgment for sin. Therefore **expect earthquakes for the following reasons: 1. The shedding of innocent blood as in the abortions of 50 million future taxpayers who could be strengthening Social Security. 2. Allowing a Muslim terrorist to kill 13 soldiers at Fort Hood, Texas and calling** such murders 'workplace violence' instead what it really was; Muslim Jihadist Terrorism. 3. The FBI forbidden to keep track of Muslim terrorists by Homeland Security so that those terrorists remained free to carry out the Boston Marathon Bombing. 4. The FBI under influence of The Muslim Brotherhood allowed a Muslim terrorist to escape to Saudi Arabia so that the Boston Marathon Bombing looked like a home grown escapade of only two local disgruntled youths. 5. The Attorney General's 'Fast and Furious' which sold guns to Mexican drug gangs to kill Mexicans now must invite in Mexican immigrants as compensation. 6. Stupid accepting of sensitivity training for the accepting of Muslims into American Society when Muslims who worship a false god here actually curse our land and invite into America all manner of evil including the degrading of women. 7. Welcoming into America all these illegal immigrants to vote Democratic (Socialist) that Deuteronomy in the Bible calls a sign of God's judgment (Deuteronomy 28:43 & 44). 8. Keeping God out of schools (no prayer or Bible reading allowed) while inviting in 'Jungle Bunnies' to push dope to your kids and contaminate them with AIDS under the guise of integration. (At least 10% of all Black males carry AIDS). This is a criminal and medical fact not racism. 9. Officially promoting GAY marriage as if such were proper and normal. 10. Homeland Security has bought up 1.6 billion bullets to deprive you of ammunition for your guns. 11. Obama Care's mandate of birth control contraceptives results in not enough future taxpayers to keep Social Security solvent. 12. Although the ego maniac Obama feels that every problem is solved by his political speeches which the psychologist call 'oral masturbation', the war on terrorism will not be over by declaring it so but by winning it.

These are just a few of the sins that I see which could cause God to move suddenly in judgment. But God is omniscient, so He sees all. I am sure that there must be other sinful issues that have offended Him.

Part of the Devine Nature includes holiness. Most Christians mistakenly believe that they can increase their own holiness by praying more or studying scripture more. While these exercises do have some merit, the prophet said that: **'To obey is better than sacrifice' (I Samuel 15:22).**

So in trying to be reconciled to become holy like Him, it's necessary to obey Him. First obey this plan of salvation. Remember that Christianity is neither a meditation of prayers from some prayer book nor a study of scriptures from some devotional book but a Person, The Lord Jesus Christ. **'He that has the Son has life; he that does not have the Son of God does not have life' (I John 5:11&12).** So ask the Lord Jesus into your heart and believe that his atoning death on the cross was His blood sacrifice that God accepts for the forgiveness of your sins. And **'because the Lord Jesus humbled himself and became obedient to death, even the death of the cross therefore God has highly exalted Him and given him a name which is above every name that at the name of Jesus every knee shall bow of things in heaven and things in earth and things under the earth. And that every tongue should confess that Jesus Christ is Lord, to the glory of God the Father' (Philippians 2:8-11).**

Then you will become 'partaker of the Divine Nature' (II Peter 1:4). And have 'the Mind of Christ'(I Corinthians 2:16). And enough common sense to move far away and not downwind from any nuclear power plant in an earthquake zone.

The awesome magnitude of the environmental catastrophe caused by earthquake and tsunami stricken nuclear power plants at Fukushima, Japan has not yet been realized. A famous 'remote viewer' (Remote viewers are secular prophets) says that this disaster may cause the eventual abandonment of the Japanese home islands and that such earthquake and tsunami phenomenon reacting with nuclear power plants could cause the extinction of our species on earth.

Of course the Lord Jesus never mentioned this catastrophe in Matthew 24 but He did say that when He comes He will make all things new. Obviously there will need to be a new earth as the one we have now will be too contaminated and polluted to live in!

Preparation

There are two kinds of preparation. The first is spiritual. Then comes the practical. Spiritual preparation is discussed by many Christian Ministers. Any Christian Minister or Missionary that's fully Christian (Pentecostal) will tell you that you need to be saved and sanctified, filled and thrilled. That is saved from the consequences of your sins by faith in confessing Jesus as your Lord. Then being buried to the old life in water (Baptized by immersion) and risen with the Lord Jesus Christ, sanctified (set apart by the Holy Ghost) to live your new life in Christ. Then filled with the Holy Ghost (baptized into Him) with the evidence of speaking in other tongues so that you may pray in the spirit and be thrilled as the Lord handles your every problem each day and gives you new 'marching orders' for each new day.

But few Christian Ministers or Missionaries mention all that the Christian needs. All Christians need to be baptized in the Holy Ghost, even you. All Christians need this not to just speak in tongues to show someone how spiritual they are, but to be able to pray in tongues (pray in the Spirit) to get Divine guidance including more information to tell you what you should do right now.

Each person's case is different. God may want you to move away or relocate. Especially if you live too close to a large body of water like the ocean. If you live at the beach you may have to move in order to avoid a storm surge from a hurricane or a tidal wave from an earthquake or landslide. But if you can't pray in tongues, you may not be able to find out what is coming your way in time enough to do something about it.

In perilous times (II Timothy 3:1) you must be able to communicate with God (to receive His 'marching orders' about how to handle daily events). Matters of life and death, like your survival requires more accurate and specific divine guidance than you might get from a prayer book or a daily devotional.

Of course it's very important to stay 'prayed up'. You need to know each day just where your neighborhood and you stand. Because you can't make all these physical preparations once the power goes out and the phones go dead. With power out ATM's will no longer work, nor can you buy anything as stores cannot open because their electric cash registers won't work.

But you probably remember that a faithless people raised under communism and atheism got delivered anyway from the Soviet menace without having to fire a shot. Many of these people did not pray. Most of them didn't even know how to pray. Nevertheless God moved decisively. As the Sovereign Lord of heaven and earth it was His prerogative to do so.

Most of these people were unarmed. But God does not need guns and bullets to enforce His will.

Being fully informed about what's coming our way we might want to follow the advice of Vice President Biden and get a shotgun for our own protection. There are also many good survival books and websites on the internet describing in detail what type of weapons for our defense that they recommend.

The American people should know by now that another civil war is being planned for by the Obama Administration. Proving this many government agencies now have their own swat team and have just purchased millions of rounds of bullets for their ammunition.

Many of these government agencies which purchased all these bullets with your tax dollars are not even involved in law enforcement. So the only reason they brought all this ammunition is to fight you.

But as Christians the weapons of our warfare are mighty through God pulling down strongholds instead.

You know how many Christian ministers and leaders exhort us to pray for our leaders. I've been doing so. And I've been praying against Obama's socialist policies that God may cast down his evil imaginations. Apparently my prayers have been working for now Obama with all his czars does not seem to know how to handle each occurring crisis.

The crisis now before us is one of a religious war (particularly with ISIS). Obama is not a fighter and obviously not even an adequate leader. He is just a deceived socialist community organizer not a warrior. His community organizing 'higher education' came from the altar of leftist icons like Alinsky, Davis and Drew all components of communist indoctrination.

Being a Black African Muslim socialist with his advisor the Iranian Valerie Jarrett, Obama has endangered Israel and the whole Middle East with nuclear assault from Iran. In order to assure the destruction of the Jewish state (Muslims like Obama hate Jews), so the Obama Administration has sent undercover American 'instigators and rebel rousers' to work against Netanyaho in the Israeli elections. Yes, this is a word of knowledge.

Here's another word of knowledge for you. I'm sure that you have heard of the neutron bomb (that kills all the people but leaves all the buildings intact). If such should have happened in the time of Joshua's conquest of the promise land all Canaanite men, women and children would have been killed by the people of God so that they could inherit houses they did not build just as the scripture says **Obama's naughtiness to this extent is not just politics but an underhanded contrivance that could offend the God of Israel to the extent that He judges America because of Obama. How's that for a political legacy: Obama equals judgment.**

Next as recorded in the Bible all these Obama infidels may just wind up killing each other with all this ammunition that they have bought with your tax dollars and we'll be delivered from them and rid of them without having to fire a shot. Nevertheless you may still want to buy Bidens' shotgun.

After you have made spiritual preparations first you are now ready for the practical preparations. First remember to keep your stress level low (by getting a de stress package by calling 1-888-988-1588) then do the following things. **Whatever the Lord tells you is coming your way, you'll need money. For 'money answers all things' (Ecclesiastes 10:19).**

But you might lack sufficient money for your needs because the government felt that financial institutions were too big to fail and so their needs were more important than your needs. So they got the money while you got food stamps and unemployment instead of being put back to work to earn a livable wage by repairing America's infrastructure.

This liberal foreign aid policy too has now become so extreme that the Democrats (who are really demagogues) feel that it is now fair to spend borrowed tax dollars that your children will have to pay back to rescue the Palestinians for four billion dollars and Afghanistan for billions more. Besides this foreign aid fiasco comes all the local expense of building code regulations and home improvement taxes for needed safety improvements like storm shelters, hurricane shutters and even fire escapes.

But if you can manage somehow to get some money on your own, then do this: buy your medications and prescription pills (at least 90 days supply). Not just for you, but for all members of your family. Then you will need a good quality Seychelle water filter in order to make into pure drinking water any polluted water you come across. Get this by calling 1-888-988-1588. Then get the silver starter kit by calling that same phone number. This is because this product kills infections from superbugs and keeps you in good health. After this get a good quality first aid kit complete with a medical information book about how to handle various medical problems. Then get at least a year's supply of healthy food. Then get a fuel less generator (solar generator) so you're prepared if the power goes down, to keep your cell phone charged up and your food cold and safe. This also is available by calling 1-888-988-1588. All of this is mainly to ensure your survival where you are now.

There are just a few things that I see that could cause God to move suddenly in judgment. But God is omniscient, so He sees all. I therefore am sure that there are many other issues that concern Him too. Just one of those concerns is about stewardship. God says in Revelation 11:18 that 'He will destroy those who destroy the earth'.

A supposedly minor issue about the die off of honey bees has now arisen. It appears that several US multinational companies are producing dangerous nicotine based pesticides that are killing the bees that we all depend upon for the pollination of our crops. If all the bees die, we die too. Einstein said we would have four years, and then the resulting famine would cause man's extinction.

You environmentalists probably thought that good stewardship of the earth was basically your concern only, and not that of some government. Especially not a communist government. But it now appears that a former Soviet Official of the former Soviet Union well remembers the disaster and disgrace of Chernobyl and how it has resulted in the contamination of mother earth in mother Russia. Now he sees the lack of honey bees poised to cause a possible famine in Russia too. And Russia does not even allow the use of these pesticides.

But this pesticide infected air swoops into Russia from Western Europe. Only 2 nations in Western Europe have outlawed this pesticide; France and Italy. He feels that it may be time to go to war to stop this pollution from happening. By the way that man happens to be Vladimir Putin the current president of Russia. This one man still controls the vastest arsenal of nuclear weapons on earth.

Who would think that something as insignificant as the honey bee could cause a war killing many millions of people. But if bees are allowed to die millions of people will die anyway because of the resulting famine.

This pesticide that's killing the bees is mainly produced by at least 3 American multinational companies. They are Bayer, Monsanto and Dow. Monsanto makes the main product called 'Round Up'.

This pesticide derived from nicotine, makes use of nicotine waste. Now that smoking has been prohibited in much of America, nicotine waste is thus being used for this poisonous product just like aluminum waste is now being used to fluoridate public drinking waters.

There is another possible cause for war right in the American Heartland. The success of the state of North Dakota in spite of the environmental insanity of the 'Food Stamp' President Obama indicates that once the people get truly informed that they don't need to settle for welfare and the expansion of welfare like Obama Care to remain dependants of the Welfare State. They will rise up and demand their basic human right to prosperity for themselves and their families.

So another civil war is on its way because of all these stupid welfare policies keeping people down and all these dumb regulations forbidding people to work and earn money for their dreams instead of earning money to pay taxes so that some bureaucrat could live 'high on the hog' at your expense.

In this case, God put the gas in the earth. And godless men forbid us to make use of it. Such governmental restrictions are anti-God and forbidden by the US Constitution which says that Congress shall make no law prohibiting the free exercise of our religious rights to receive the bounty of blessing the Lord wants us to have. Those that don't want us to have these blessing are akin to perverts who won't let us give CPR to some victim because of the groundless fear of air pollution from bad breath.

Yes war is on its way and although I didn't even sufficiently discuss the Middle East Crisis because of my orders from God to cut the length of my book in order to get its warning out quickly.

Nevertheless our brother Bill Salus in his book: **Psalm 83 The Missing Prophecy Revealed** discusses some of what needs to be said about the destruction of Damascus. (Damascus according to Isaiah 17 is a capitol city at the time of its destruction. And it did not become a capitol city in modern times until 1946 when it received its independence from France).

There are also other major end time truths which I should comment on. Like when will the Rapture of the Church occur. But these things are adequately discussed already by our brother John Shorey in his book: **The Window of the Lords Return 2012-2020**.

In this case I'll follow the example of our brother, the Evangelist Jimmy Swaggart. Although he is an experienced and recorded professional singer, he stands back for others to use their gifting and anointing to sing. This works out well for others sing what he feels needs to be expressed for the glory of God.

Some of my readers may be Obama supporters. If so, this truth is for you. There is no need for the United States to begin another expensive major war in the Middle East. Particularly in enforcing a no fly zone over Syria to start with. Where Syria is concerned the battle is not ours but God's. So it would be stupid to aid the Muslim Brotherhood any more after what they got away with in North Africa. Damascus is going to be destroyed, Bible Prophecy says so (Isaiah 17:1). So let's face it and accept it and stay ready for the real war that's coming.

Our brother Hal Lindsey says on page 197 of his book: **Planet Earth–2000AD** that 'there is no question in reviewing Bible Prophecy, that a cataclysmic, apocalyptic war will engulf the Middle East prior to the return of Jesus Christ'. But this war does not need to be our own. Another war is coming involving the Anti-Christ, and before that we've got problems in America that may require the dispensing of some social justice right here. To stop Illegal Immigration and their unfunded mandates to educate illegals causing teacher firings. To stop feeding your school kids genetically modified foods. To stop requiring the unemployed to buy Obama Care. To stop unemployment due to environmental insanity. And to stop the planned stealing of your IRA's to fund government waste.

Moreover our brother, the Prophet Roberts Liardon says in his book on **Spiritual Timing** that 'A time of conflict, a time of war has the Church come into. This is not a time of peace'. Then he says what all evangelicals believe: **'Warfare is always a precedence for spiritual harvest'. So another revival is possible, 'with God all things are possible' Matthew 19:26.**

In that vein of truth let me share my prophecy of worship with you. **'The Lord Jesus Christ is that Light that lights every man that comes into the World. His countenance is more dazzling than diamonds sparkling. His image is more majestic than gold shimmering in the sunlight of noonday. His presence permeates all like silver molten in the fiery furnace. By Him were all things made, and through Him do all things consist. And He upholds all by the Word of His awesome power. Holy, Holy, Holy, Lord, God, Almighty, which were, and are, and are to come. Heaven and earth are filled with your glory. Hosanna'!**

As these words infuse and envelope your spirit, You may feel that this is a nice evangelical word. But I am not a nicey-nicey feel good evangelist. But a no-nonsense street prophet. But as with all prophecy, **'we know in part and prophecy in part' (I Corinthians 13:9).** So some things may happen as predicted. But since God is the Sovereign Lord He can change His mind as to Him revival is much better than judgment.

So when Jonah prophesied against Nineveh in your Bible God sent revival instead of deserved judgment because the people repented after hearing Jonah's word from God. Jonah was not a false prophet nor were his words untrue but because of repentance, God sent revival instead of judgment. Such could happen again and if so. **Praise God!**

Most Christians are looking forward to the second coming of the Lord Jesus in power and great glory. But before he comes again, the Bible says that other important events must occur first. One of these is the falling away from the faith in Christ. Another one is the Revelation of the man of sin, or Antichrist. The next ones concern Israel since the times of the gentiles have been fulfilled.

Since there has been no repentance since 9 11. I have just received this revelation for America, Israel and you: **'The time of America's judgment has come. There will be a great shaking in America for it has turned away from God. As America falls Israel will begin to rise by wars that it will win. In one of these wars Damascus will be destroyed (Isaiah 17). Then it will be realized that this means Total War (Zachariah 14:12). In the Total War of the U.S. Civil War Sherman burned Atlanta and shot those civilians who would not leave.**

Before I get to my final prophecy, I'll lay a few 'words of knowledge' on you. I'm sure that you have heard about the neutron bomb that's used in total war. That kills all the people (men, women and children) but leaves the buildings intact. Of course the liberals hated this because to them it was the same as genocide. In fact when George H.W. Bush (Bush 41) was president of the USA he not only lied when he said: 'read my lips, no new taxes'. But also listened to the liberals and raised taxes instead. And also removed from America's arsenal the neutron bomb since the liberals wanted him to do so.

So now with no neutron bombs in America's arsenal George W. Bush (Bush 43) was forced to send American troops into hand to hand combat in Iraq. So just as I told you before that most every city and town in America now has a population of far less men than woman. Plus as a result of this Iraq war Bush 43 has imported into America over a million Iraqi Muslims.

Now the Muslim Obama has also imported into America a million Syrian refugees (Muslims) even though it is common knowledge that Muslims curse the land that they occupy (most Muslim lands are cursed deserts from North Africa to the Middle East). This was done as the Muslim Obama listened to his Muslim advisor; Valerie Jarrett who wants to make America a Muslim nation.

This of course brings my final prophecy into play for as I said before this war is to be a total war. When Joshua conquered the promised land he was told by God to kill everyone (men women and children) of the reprobate Canaanites that the Jews might inhabit houses that they did not build.

Likewise 'whosoever that does not worship and honor the God of Israel according to the Old Testament or the God of Israel according to the New Testament shall be driven out of My land by force. Do not let the stupid mindset of diversity (worship of false gods like those of Jihadist Muslims) deceive you as 'freedom of religion' destroyed America. As the Muslims go destroy their Mosques. Israel will expand to the original borders that I gave her in my covenant with Abraham. But if Israel does not drive out the inhabitants of My land and destroy their Mosques they shall also fail to obey My Commandment; 'Thou shalt have no other God's before Me'. And you know what that means'. This is the word of the Lord. Thanks be to God for His coming year of Jubilee.

Twenty

Back in the 1970's I was one of the five fold ministry at the Maranatha House here in Daytona Beach, Florida. Our other ministers were: Reverend Earl Warren. He had been an Associate Pastor of White Chapel Church of God in South Daytona, Florida. And was now our Pastor. About his same age was our Bible teacher named Rollin Emmonds. Rollin was also a 'dirt farmer' who owned his own plant nursery. He possessed a lot of the spiritual gift called: 'The word of wisdom'. And was somewhat like Charles Capps, the folksy radio minister from England, Arkansas. Our next minister was a spiritual man named Warren Houser who seemed to operate in apostolic authority. Our evangelist, about my same age back then, was a young man named: Jon Morris from California. Then I operated in the congregational gift of prophecy but would also teach occasionally. Although all of us were considered spiritual leaders of the New Testament Church in Daytona back then, we also attended (but did not rule over) different Bible study groups in town.

One evening some of us went to hear a new minister from California, to see what God was giving him for us. He taught a Bible study about some topic that I no longer remember. Although I forgot the main theme, I still remember this: for some reason the number twenty came up. And he went on to mention that in ancient Israel a young Hebrew had to be at least twenty years old in order to fight in the army of God. And that the number twenty usually indicates or means that war is at hand.

Consequently I have now given you twenty points to Obama's Muslim deception and twenty issues about the Muslim Jesus verses Jesus Christ. Plus twenty chapters of my prophetic book to now make it clear to you prophetically to expect war for it's coming your way.

The Bible says that a threefold cord is not easily broken

(Ecclesiastes 4:12). So when a warning, like this is three fold you should certainly know to expect and prepare for it.

Although most of my book has now been completed with my last prophecy, whenever an author writes a book he discovers by research things that need to be said. In that light let me give to the nations a public service for your benefit.

First the United States of America should impeach its Muslim President Barack Obama for the many valid and self evident reasons listed in my prophetic book. The following final clear reason may help you get rid of this 'wolf in sheep's clothing':

I am sure that you have seen over TV News where President Obama calls ISIS ISIL. Here is what that means: ISIS is the Islamic State in Iraq and Syria. But ISIL is a Muslim boast about the Islamic State conquering the whole region and becoming a Middle Eastern Muslim Caliphate ruling over Jordan, Israel and Lebanon too. Only a radical Muslim would dare to use such an expression which is an insult to the free nations composing that region.

For those of you who say that the Muslim Obama has no strategy of dealing with ISIS: a strategy to lose or betray, instead of a strategy to win is still a strategy. Now isn't it? And you just saw it with your own eyes on TV. Wakeup America!

Now when you throw this Muslim Obama out with him also throw out all the Muslim enemies of America that the Muslim Obama invited into America to squat on us at our expense too.

Let me further say that Islam is not a true religion at all. For all the world's religions are concerned about how to get ready to live better in heaven. So, to take carnal human attributes like sexual feelings from having sex with 73 virgins and apply that to eternal life in heaven is a form of psychological dysfunction known as anthropomorphism.

From their Quran (Koran) we know that Muslims believe that Christians and Jews are apes and pigs. But non-Muslims like you are also infidels 'made to be taken and destroyed'.

No ideology that glorifies death like Islam could possibly lead to an eternal life worth living in heaven. The Bible says in **Isaiah 55:8, 9 'My thoughts are not your thoughts, neither are your ways My ways'** declares the Lord. **'As the heavens are higher than the earth so are My ways than your ways'.**

Moreover the Bible also says in **Romans 6:23** that **'the wages of sin are death'** not an eternal life of having sex with 73 virgins! Muslims need to get real, a new life with God is for new experiences in God and these only come through the Lord Jesus Christ, the Son of the living God!

Now let me move on to the Black African nations ruled by both dictators and elected presidents; for your own good do not allow Muslims especially Black Muslims to gain a foothold in your respective countries. Because Islam is not a religion of peace but a totalitarian ideology of conquest.

Let me further say that Islam is not a true religion at all. For all the world's religions are concerned about how to get ready to live better in heaven. So, to take carnal human attributes like sexual feelings from having sex with 73 virgins and apply that to eternal life in heaven is a form of psychological dysfunction known as anthropomorphism.

From their Quran (Koran) we know that Muslims believe that Christians and Jews are apes and pigs. But non-Muslims like you are also infidels 'made to be taken and destroyed'.

No ideology that glorifies death like Islam could possibly lead to an eternal life worth living in heaven. The Bible says in **Isaiah 55:8, 9 'My thoughts are not your thoughts, neither are your ways My ways'** declares the Lord. **'As the heavens are higher than the earth so are My ways than your ways'.**

Moreover the Bible also says in **Romans 6:23** that **'the wages of sin are death'** not an eternal life of having sex with 73 virgins! Muslims need to get real, a new life with God is for new experiences in God and these only come through the Lord Jesus Christ, the Son of the living God!

Muslims feel that any government not part of their Muslim Caliphate is illegitimate. So they employ terrorist guerilla tactics to overthrow your governments. Such as the kidnapping of school children (girls) to rape and then sell into sexual slavery.

To you European nations ruled by Sovereigns (Kings and Queens) and social Democracies do not allow Muslims to gain a foothold in your countries by hiding their ultimate objective of conquest of your society under your freedom of religion rights. As I said before, Islam is not a religion of peace but a totalitarian ideology of conquest in favor of the establishment through war of their Muslim Caliphate. Remember their rebellious incidents of mayhem, riot and bombing. And their black flag of Isis and brutality as signs of the Islamic Antichrist. To open your eyes you should read that book: <u>The Islamic Antichrist</u> by Joel Richardson.

Let me further say that Islam is not a true religion at all. For all the world's religions are concerned about how to get ready to live better in heaven. So, to take carnal human attributes like sexual feelings from having sex with 73 virgins and apply that to eternal life in heaven is a form of psychological dysfunction known as anthropomorphism.

From their Quran (Koran) we know that Muslims believe that Christians and Jews are apes and pigs. But non-Muslims like you are also infidels 'made to be taken and destroyed'.

No ideology that glorifies death like Islam could possibly lead to an eternal life worth living in heaven. The Bible says in **Isaiah 55:8, 9 'My thoughts are not your thoughts, neither are your ways My ways'** declares the Lord. **'As the heavens are higher than the earth so are My ways than your ways'.**

Moreover the Bible also says in **Romans 6:23** that **'the wages of sin are death'** not an eternal life of having sex with 73 virgins! Muslims need to get real, a new life with God is for new experiences in God and these only come through the Lord Jesus Christ, the Son of the living God!

To you Communist Rulers do not allow Muslims to gain any foothold in your countries for they believe less in human rights than you do. And intend to mistreat and abuse your own people as should be evident from their killing of your school children in Russia and abuse of the People's Government of China.

Back in 1947 British India was dissolved into two nations: Muslim Pakistan and Hindu India. This independence was brought about by Gandhi the pacifist lawyer. Although it was agreed back then that the Muslims would leave India for Pakistan, many stayed particularly in Kashmir, India where they have been causing trouble all these years.

It's time to quit being pacifist and go to the World Court like any competent lawyer would to get the original colonial agreement confirmed. Then India needs to enforce that decision, for India has too many hungry people to allow the reprehensible presence of Muslims upon it to turn India's land into a God forsaken desert, just like other Muslim lands.

Index of issues

Printed in the United States
By Bookmasters